MOTIVATION

McGraw-Hill Programmed Series in Psychology
(El Pro Series)

Smith/Moore CONDITIONING AND INSTRUMENTAL LEARNING
Teevan/Smith MOTIVATION
Manning/Rosenstock CLASSICAL PSYCHOPHYSICS AND SCALING (WITH
PREFACE AND AFTERWORD BY DOUGLAS K. CANDLAND,
TO BE PUBLISHED IN 1967).
Brookshire/Stewart PHYSIOLOGICAL PSYCHOLOGY (TO BE PUBLISHED)
OTHER UNITS IN THIS SERIES WILL BE ANNOUNCED AS PUBLISHED.

MOTIVATION

RICHARD C. TEEVAN
Professor of Psychology, Bucknell University

BARRY D. SMITH
University of Massachusetts

McGRAW-HILL BOOK COMPANY
New York   St. Louis   San Francisco   Toronto   London   Sydney

MOTIVATION

1 2 3 4 5 6 7 8 9 0 MR 7 4 3 2 1 0 6 9 8 7

Editor's Introduction

The units in this series have arisen from two trends in the field of elementary psychology. The first is the trend toward the use of separate books for each component part of the field of psychology. Many instructors find a single text too confining. They would like to have greater selectivity in the topics they cover in their courses and would like more variability in the way these topics are handled. The second trend is that toward independent work in the elementary course. Those who have taught and researched in this trend have looked for materials which the student could cover by himself with little or no contact with the teacher. Materials such as these can be used in independent work, but also can free the instructor to adopt his class hours in his own uses, confident that the basic information of the course has been covered and understood.

In this series we have asked authors who are expert in the various sub-fields of psychology to write introductions to these sub-fields in individual books. Each book corresponds to a topic which would usually be covered in a chapter or two in a standard elementary textbook. Usually the material covered in a book in the series will go beyond the standard coverage. This allows the instructor to choose the topics he wishes to cover in his course, to cover them a little more deeply, and to get the coverage of a sub-field by an expert in that subfield. A major departure of this series is that each of the volumes will be programmed. This technique insures that the student who goes through the material will understand it. Each of the volumes has been, or will be, well-tested so that we will know that the error rate in each book will be small and also we will know that completion of the program will be equivalent to understanding the material in the program. Thus these volumes will be ideal for independent study.

The instructor may choose among the volumes in this series in order to make up a course. He may also use a standard text but use books in this series as supplements—he may want some additional coverage of a particular topic or he may not intend to cover a particular topic in class and may therefore want to make sure that that topic will be understood without class help.

In summary: this is a unique series of programmed textbooks which is designed for the elementary course in psychology. Each book will be written by an expert in the sub-field concerned. Each program will be tested for error rate and understanding. These volumes should be useful together as substituting for a standard elementary text or singly as supplements to such a text.

Richard C. Teevan, General Editor
Bucknell University

Preface

A primary goal of psychology as a science is the prediction of behavior. Therefore, any field of study which contributes to such prediction is of value to psychology.

It is generally agreed among psychologists that the study of motivation fulfills this criterion. In order to predict behavior, it is first necessary to know, among other things, why the behavior occurs when it does. It is the "why" of behavior to which the psychology of motivation provides a partial answer. Why does a rat seek food? Why does one college student work very hard to become an engineer, while another does little or no work? The answer to the first question seems obvious—the rat is hungry. The answer to the second is not so clear, for the motivation of each student is determined by a variety of past and present factors and is usually very complex. The important point is that the psychology of motivation seeks the why of both simple and complex behavior, especially insofar as knowledge of the former provides clues to the latter. It seeks the why, in fact, of all behavior and thus aids psychology in the prediction of behavior.

Motivation studies an even more basic question than that of specific motives. Why is the organism active at all? Why does it exert itself? Why does it not simply remain quiescent? The general answer provided by the psychology of motivation is that the organism is *motivated* to be active. This, however, is a far-from-adequate answer, since it provides no real answer to the question. A more adequate answer is that behavior is activated by a number of specific motives, such as hunger and thirst. Even the explanation that the rat seeks food because of a hunger motive is not adequate unless an adequate definition of hunger and some details concerning the operation of a hunger motive can be provided.

The importance of studying motivation lies not only in its contribution to the prediction of behavior but also in the fact that it permeates every aspect of daily living. The mother is concerned with what motivates her child to cry. The shop foreman and his superiors are interested in how best to motivate employees to higher production. The criminal court is concerned with what motivated a particular criminal to kill and in general with what motives underly crimes. The educator is concerned with motivating students to learn. And the individual is often interested in what has motivated a superior, a friend, or an enemy to perform a particular act.

Although the study of motivation is a relatively young branch of psychology, its importance has been recognized for some time, and the topic is covered in most introductory texts. The present text provides a systematic and somewhat more thorough coverage than do most introductory texts. Its programmed format makes it especially useful in courses where independent study is used. Since it is an introduction to motivation, it requires no previous knowledge of psychology.

Richard C. Teevan
Barry D. Smith

Instructions for the Use of the Text

As you probably know, this is a programmed text. This means it is designed not only to present the material to be learned but actually to help you learn it. The latter aim is accomplished by applying certain principles of the psychology of learning. Thus, the program presents the material in small, logically sequenced units, requires you to make an active (written) response to each unit, provides you with immediate knowledge of whether or not your response is correct, and repeats important concepts to aid you in learning them.

Each chapter is divided into small numbered units called frames. Each frame consists of one or more statements, usually containing blanks which you are to fill in. Correct answers are presented next to each frame. The frames will be of five major types:

1. Frames with blanks to be filled in. Usually (but not always) the number of blanks will give you a clue as to the number of words to be filled in. You should, however, know the answer without the necessity for this clue in most cases.

2. Matching frames, in which you will be asked to match a cer-

tain set of concepts to a number of statements about the concepts.

3. Classification frames, in which you will be asked to classify a number of statements as referring to one or more of several concepts discussed in earlier frames.

4. Selection frames, in which two or more alternative answers will be given and you will be asked to choose one.

5. Review frames, in which you will be asked to review one or more concepts in your own words, to state a definition, or to give an answer requiring more than one or two words.

At some points there are rather lengthy sections of discourse which are not broken up into frames. You should simply read these sections carefully, noting particularly the important concepts and their ramifications. Each discourse will then be followed by a series of frames which provide questions and give further examples to clarify the material.

In reading the text, it is important that you respond to each blank in each frame before looking at the correct answer. It is best actually to *write* your answers in the blanks provided or on a separate sheet of paper before looking at the correct answers. When you check your answers against the correct ones, you will find it profitable to mark those that you initially missed; then, go back to those frames at a later time and again attempt to answer the questions. If you fail a second time, reread the relevant material to discover where your difficulty lies.

The exemplary frames which follow, and those in the General Introduction (pp. xviii and xix) contain no actual blanks. However, words which might have been left as blanks are italicized and enclosed in parentheses. You should read these frames carefully for practice before beginning the text itself.

1. The numbered units into which each chapter is divided are called (*frames*). These frames aid in learning partly because they require an (*active*) response.

2. Fill-in, matching, classification, selection, and review are the five types of (*frames*). Match these five types with the following definitions by placing the name of one type in each blank:

(1) Frames in which a choice of answers is given (*selection*)

(2) Frames which involve completing a statement (*fill-in*)

(3) Frames in which concepts are to be categorized (*classification*)

(4) Frames in which you are to state a definition (*review*)

(5) The type of frame on which you are now working (*matching*)

3. Frame 1 above is an example of a (*fill-in*) (fill-in, selection) frame. This frame (3) is a (*selection*) (fill-in, selection) frame.

4. What is the best procedure to follow when you miss an answer?

5. Classify each of the above four frames and the present one as to type of frame by placing the proper name beside the frame numbers which follow:

(1) (*fill-in*)

(2) (*matching and fill-in*)

(3) (*selection*)

(4) (*review*)

(5) (*classification*)

The programmed chapters of this text have been tested on a number of students and have been found to do a very satisfactory job of teaching the material found in the chapters. If you follow the instructions given above, you should be able to learn the material without difficulty.

Contents

Two primary concerns of psychology are the prediction and modification of behavior. But in order to predict or modify behavior, psychologists must first know what some of the underlying determinants of behavior are and how these determinants operate to influence behavior.

More basic than the question of specific determinants is the question of why the organism behaves at all. Why is a normal animal active a major proportion of the time? Why doesn't the animal simply remain quiescent? In order to answer this basic question and its ramifications, we must postulate that something moves this organism, something activates it and directs it to perform specific functions, such as seeking and eating food, drinking, and avoiding pain. The broad construct which psychologists have postulated to account for the activation of behavior is *motivation,* and the more specific components of motivation relating to particular types of behavior have been termed *motives.*

The study of motivation is not exclusively the domain of the psychologist. It is, in fact, of such widespread concern as to be of importance to any individual who must deal with other people. A mother must determine what motivates the infant to cry on a particular occasion. Is it hunger, thirst, discomfort, pain? The businessman is necessarily concerned with the factors that will motivate his employees to maximal productivity. The educator is concerned with the motivation of students. Why does one college student spend long hours at his desk while another spends most of his time at extracurricular activities? The salesman and his employer are extremely interested in consumer motivation. What features do people like in a product? How best can they be motivated to buy one brand over another brand of the same product? Our legal system is likewise concerned with the motives behind behavior. The verdict in a case of premeditated murder is likely to be quite different from that in a case of self-defense. These are only a few examples of the importance of gaining a knowledge of human motivation.

An attempt to approach such a broad topic as motivation without adequate narrowing and directing influences could only end in confusion. It will therefore be helpful to formulate several more specific (though still broad) questions which motivational psychology has attempted to deal with. Some of the questions which have been of primary concern are the following:

1. Can most motives be classified into broad categories? That is, do certain kinds of motives have properties in common?

The answer to this question is "yes," so far as most psychologists are concerned. Some motives, for example, are physiological; that is, they are based on the physiological needs of the organism. The hunger motive or *drive* is aroused by a need for food, thirst by a need for water, etc. Other motives are nonphysiological. The college student's drive to become a football star or an engineer is a nonphysiological motive. All *social* motives are now generally considered to come under the nonphysiological classification. Various other classification systems for categorizing motives are also possible. Some of these will be discussed in later chapters.

2. How do motives operate?

This question actually has two aspects. First, how is the motive aroused? Secondly, how does the motive, once aroused, activate behavior? It seems obvious that the hunger motive is aroused by a need for food, and thirst by a need for liquid. This explanation, however, is merely an extension of the definition of these motives. The real question is *how* the need for food arouses the hunger motive. What is the mechanism or process of arousal? Although some tentative answers have been found for the relatively simple hunger and thirst drives, the question is a more difficult one when it involves the more complex social motives.

A related problem is whether or not there are certain consistencies in the modes of operation of various motives. The attempted solution of this problem has led to the development of a number of *motivational theories*. A basic assumption of all these theories is that there *are* certain principles which govern the operation of large groups of motives. Each theory represents an attempt to state some of the general principles underlying motivation. As we shall see later, a number of theoretical viewpoints have attempted to account for motivated behavior with varying degrees of success.

3. Are motives innate (present at birth) or are they acquired through experience and learning?

This question has been of major concern to a number of theorists and to experimental psychologists studying motivated behavior. It has no simple answer. In part, the answer is that some motives are probably innate and others are learned. However, this is by no means the whole solution.

OVERVIEW AND PREVIEW

The three questions discussed above are certainly not the only problems in the study of motivation. They do, however, represent some of the primary reasons for much of the theory and research carried out in this area. In the chapters which follow, we will discuss in some detail the partial answers which have been found or at least offered to these and other questions concerning motivation. We will discuss the classification and operation of motives in general and then take up the topic of specific motives, moving from the relatively simple to the more complex motives. At each point we will note the important problems which have been raised and the solutions which have been offered. In addition, we will be concerned with the research which has led to particular solutions and will discuss some of this research in detail. Finally, we will discuss some of the major theoretical viewpoints which have attempted to tie together the variety of research results.

1. The construct postulated to account for the activity of organisms is called (*motivation*).

2. The specific components of motivation which relate to particular types of behavior are called (*motives*).

3. Hunger and thirst are both (*motives*), since they cause the organism to be active.

4. Most psychologists agree that motives can be (*classified*) into broad categories within which the various motives have some property in common.

5. One classification system categorized motives as (*physiological*) and (*nonphysiological*). An example of a motive in the first of these categories is (*sex*) (in the second, the drive to obtain money).

6. A physiological motive is one which is based on the physiological (*needs*) of the organism. A nonphysiolgical motive (*is not*) (is, is not) based on these (*needs*).

7. Give an example of:
    (*a*) A physiological motive (*hunger, thirst, sex*)
    (*b*) A nonphysiological motive (*desire to be an engineer, to obtain money, etc.*)

8. One of the primary questions with which motivational psychologists are concerned is how motives (*operate*). Two aspects of this question are how the (*motive*) is *aroused* and how it *activates* (*behavior*).

9. Both the businessman who works far into the night to solve a problem and the rat which presses a bar to obtain food are (*motivated*). The specific (*motives*) underlying the behaviors are, however, undoubtedly different.

10. A basic assumption underlying all theories of motivation is that certain general (*principles*) govern the operation of large groups of motives.

11. It seems probable that some motives are *innate* while others are (*acquired*).
        learned

12. Classify each of the following as physiological or nonphysiological by writing the proper letter in the blank:
    (*a*) Hunger (*P*)
    (*b*) Sex (*P*)

    (*c*) Desire to be a medical doctor (*N*)

    (*d*) Thirst (*P*)

    (*e*) Avoiding an electric shock (*P*)

    13. State briefly three major questions which have guided the thinking of psychologists studying motivation (see pages xvi and xvii for answers). The above practice frames have contained no actual blanks, but, rather, the answers are italicized and placed in parentheses. For the remainder of the text, however, blanks will be present in most frames. You should always attempt to fill in the blanks before looking at the answers given in the right margin.

Introduction 1

The terms *motive* and *drive* have been variously defined by a number of theorists and experimenters interested in studying the psychology of motivation. Although some psychologists have distinguished between motives and drives by indicating that the former are learned and the latter unlearned, we shall not, for present purposes, make this distinction. Instead, we shall use the two terms synonymously.

Various investigators have also attributed different functions to motives. Here, we shall define motives as having two primary properties. First, a motive or drive *energizes* or *activates* behavior. That is, the presence of a drive, such as hunger or thirst, causes the organism experiencing the drive to become active. Second, motives *direct* behavior. This guiding function is exemplified by the specific types of behavior engaged in by a motivated organism. Thus, the hungry animal seeks food, the thirsty animal water. It has been hypothesized that the directive function of motives is based on specific internal stimuli called *drive stimuli* and that it is these drive stimuli which actually direct motivated behavior.

1.1 A *motive* or *drive* is an *energizer* or activator of behavior. Since thirst activates the organism to behavior, thirst can be a

motive
(drive)

_____.

1.2 When an organism is thirsty, we can say that the organism is _____.

motivated

energizes
(activates)

1.3 Thirst is called a drive partly because it _____ the organism.

1.4 Associated with each drive which _____ the organism are *internal stimuli* which indicate to the organism which drive is active. Thirst, for example, is accompanied by *dryness* of the mouth and throat.

energizes

internal

1.5 The _____ stimuli which accompany a drive are called *drive stimuli*. These *drive stimuli* are thought to *direct* the behavior of the organism.

1.6 We can therefore state that a second property associated with motivation is that of *direction*. This guiding function of the motive will cause the animal motivated by thirst to move in the _____ of water.

direction

stimuli

1.7 Many psychologists hypothesize that a motive does not itself direct behavior. Instead the drive _____ closely associated with the motive guide the behavior. The dryness of the mouth and throat specifically associated with thirst are _____ _____ for the thirst motive.

drive stimuli

1.8 The drive stimuli associated with another

motive, hunger, include stomach contractions. When these contractions occur in
connection with the hunger motive, we
say that they _____ the orga-   direct
nism toward food.

1.9   The two principal properties associ-   activation
      ated with motivation are, then, the   (energizing)
      _____ and the _____   direction
      of behavior.

1.10 Behavior which is activated or energized
      by the hunger motive is directed toward
      food by the _____ _____   drive stimuli
      associated with hunger.

1.10a State the two principal properties of
      motives.
      (1) _____   (1) activation
      (2) _____   (2) direction

1.10b What is the mechanism through which
      motivated behavior is directed?
      _____   drive stimuli

THE MOTIVATIONAL SEQUENCE

There is, of course, a wide variety of behavior which may be said to
be motivated, and hence there are a number of different motives. Some
have a largely physiological basis. Examples include hunger, thirst, sex,
and pain. Others, such as social motives, are thought to be largely
nonphysiological and are based on the learning and experience of the
organism.

How can such widely different behavioral antecedents all be referred to as motives? One answer is that all conform to the basic
definition of a motive as having energizing and directing functions. A
second answer is that all these diverse behavioral antecedents operate
in basically the same manner, in that all are patterned or *sequential*.

The *motivational sequence* has four principal components or steps.

The first is the *antecedent condition,* which may be either a need or a stimulus, the former being a deficiency or lack, such as a need for food, the latter being something which impinges on the organism from the environment or from within. The second component is the *motive* or *drive* itself, which has been defined previously. The third step is *instrumental behavior.* This is the specific activity in which the organism engages in an effort to reduce the drive. The final component of the motivational sequence is *drive* reduction, which is accomplished by reaching a *goal,* such as food. As the term implies, the goal reduces or temporarily alleviates the drive.

A further characteristic which cuts across most or all motives is that the motivational sequence associated with a particular drive tends to be repeated with each occurrence of the need on which that drive is based. Motives are thus said to be *cyclical,* the cycle being repeated with each presentation of a given stimulus or need.

1.11 Although there are a number of different motives or drives (hunger, thirst, sex, social drives, etc.), most can be said to conform to a regular pattern or *sequence.* Since hunger is a motive, we can say that the events associated with hunger are

sequential
(patterned)

_____.

1.12 The *motivational sequence* consists of four principal components or steps: *antecedent condition, motive* or *drive, instrumental response,* and *drive reduction.*

1.13 The *antecedent condition* may be either a *need* or a *stimulus.* The need or stimulus constitutes the first step in the

motivational

_____ sequence.

1.14 A *need* is a *deficiency* or lack of something needed by the organism. It often occurs when the organism has been *deprived* of a particular necessity. When a rat is experimentally deprived of food for

forty-eight hours, it will probably develop
a _____ for food.

need

1.15 When we wish to create a need for food
in the rat, we _____ the rat of
food for a period of time.

deprive

1.16 For some types of motives, the second
type of antecedent condition, the
s_____, acts in conjunction
with or in place of the need.

stimulus

1.17 Hunger pangs are one example of an internal _____ acting in conjunc-
tion with a need. Electric shock is an
example of a _____ acting in
place of a need.

stimulus

stimulus

1.18 The first step in the motivational sequence
thus consists of a stimulus or a
_____, either of which is an
_____ condition for the arousal
of a motive.

need

antecedent

1.19 The second component of the sequence is
the *motive* or *drive* which is aroused by
the _____ or _____.

need, stimulus

1.20 When the rat is deprived of food, the
need thus created arouses the hunger
_____, which activates the
organism and causes it to engage in
instrumental behavior. This behavior is
so called because it is instrumental in reducing the drive.

motive
(drive)

1.21 The action taken by the organism in response to the activation of a drive is
called i_____ b_____.

instrumental
behavior

A rat motivated by hunger will learn to turn right (or left) in a T-maze in order to get food. The food is thus the goal of the instrumental behavior, and the latter is said to be *goal-directed* behavior.

1.22 A primary characteristic of instrumental behavior is that it is directed toward a _____ and is therefore _____ - _____ behavior. The goal is something which will satisfy or *reduce* the drive.

goal
goal-directed

1.23 The last step in the motivational sequence, drive reduction, occurs when the organism reaches the goal. The food which is the _____ of the rat's instrumental behavior _____ the hunger drive.

goal
reduces

1.24 A thirsty animal will seek water because water _____ the drive. The drive is not, however, *eliminated*, or removed, but only temporarily _____.

reduces

reduced

1.25 Since the drive is not permanently _____ by the attainment of the goal, it can and does recur. The motivational sequence is therefore *cyclical*.

eliminated
(reduced)

1.26 The fact that a rat whose hunger drive has been reduced will repeat the motivational sequence if deprived is evidence that motivation is _____.

cyclical

1.27 The frequent need for food expressed by the infant's cries is another example of the cyclical nature of _____

motivation

and of the fact that a drive is not elimi-
nated but only temporarily _____.   reduced

1.27a What is the result of "successful" instrumental behavior? _____   drive reduction

1.28 The drive aroused by the presention of
electric shock is an example of a drive,
the antecedent condition of which is a
_____ rather than a need.   stimulus
Since this drive, like hunger or thirst,
causes the organism to engage in instrumental behavior which will reduce the
drive, it also can be said to follow the
usual motivational _____.   sequence

1.29 The general rule is that the motivational
sequence associated with a particular
motive is likely to be repeated whenever
the _____ or _____   need, stimulus
associated with that motive is present.
Motivation is therefore said to be

_____.   cyclical

1.30 The four major steps in the motivational   (1) antecedent
sequence are: (1) the _____   condition
_____, (2) the _____,   (2) motive
(3) _____ _____,   (3) instrumental
and (4) _____ _____.   behavior
                                                             (4) drive
                                                                  reduction

1.30a For each of the following terms and
phrases, write the step in the motivational
sequence to which the term or phrase is   instrumental
most closely related or of which it is   behavior
most descriptive.   motive
Seeking food   _____   need (antecedent
Thirst   _____   condition)

motive	Lack of food	_____
drive reduction	Hunger	_____
stimulus	Eating food	_____
instrumental	Electric shock	_____
behavior	Running from shock	_____

REINFORCEMENT

When certain events following a response of the organism increase the likelihood or *probability* that the same response will occur again in the same situation, the events are said to be *reinforcers*. Thus, food given to a rat for pressing a bar will increase the probability of bar pressing. The food is, therefore, a reinforcer. The statement that reinforcement occurs whenever response probability increases when the response is followed by a particular event is called the *empirical law of effect*.

Reinforcers are of two major types, *positive* and *negative,* the former being one which the organism approaches, the latter one which it avoids. Hence, food is a positive reinforcer, and electric shock a negative reinforcer.

1.31 When an organism's hunger is reduced by the attainment of food, the food is a *reinforcer* which is said to *reinforce* the particular *response* that immediately preceded the presentation of the food.

reinforces   1.32 The food _____ the response which immediately precedes its presentation, and it becomes more likely or more *probable* that the same response will recur when the organism is again placed in that situation.

1.33 If a rat deprived of food for forty-eight hours is placed in a box containing a lever and discovers that when the lever is pressed it will receive a food reward, the rat will *learn* to press the lever repeatedly. This is probably because the food

_____ the response of press-   reinforces
ing the lever.

1.34 It is generally agreed that *reinforcement*
occurs whenever an event following a
response increases the *probability* that
that response will recur in that situation.
This statement is called the *empirical law
of effect*. Thus, when the rat's bar-pressing
response increases in probability following presentation of food, it can be said
that _____ has occurred.   reinforcement

1.35 An event which increases the probability
of a particular response in a given situation is a *reinforcer*. When a water-
deprived rat learns to press a bar for
water, the bar-pressing response is
_____ by water, which is a   reinforced
_____.   reinforcer

1.36 Reinforcement involves an increase in the
_____ of occurrence of a par-   probability
ticular response.

1.37 The statement that _____ will   reinforcement
increase the probability of occurrence of
a response is called the _____   empirical law
_____ _____.   of effect

1.38 Most reinforcers can be conveniently
divided into *positive* and *negative* reinforcers. A *positive* reinforcer is one
which the animal *approaches*; a *negative*
reinforcer is one which the organism will
learn to avoid or escape. Both types increase the _____ of a response.   probability

1.39 Since a hungry rat will learn to press a

positive

reinforcer
approaches
negative

increase

law of
  effect

empirical
positive
negative

reinforcement

Reinforcement
  will increase
  the prob-
  ability of
  occurrence
  of a response.

bar in order to get food, the food is a (positive, negative) reinforcer.

1.40 While food is a positive _____ because the rat _____ it, electric shock is a _____ reinforcer since the rat will attempt to avoid or escape from it.

1.41 The probability of a rat's bar-pressing response will _____ if this response avoids the onset of shock. This is an example of the operation of the empirical _____ _____ _____.

1.42 The _____ law of effect holds for both _____ and _____ reinforcers.

1.43 The operation which increases the probability of a particular response in a given situation is called _____.

1.44 We should note that although *drive reduction* is a *sufficient* condition for the occurrence of reinforcement, it may or may not be a *necessary* one. There are, in fact, some prominent psychological theories that hypothesize that drive reduction is necessary and others that hold that it is not.

1.44a State the empirical law of effect.

_____
_____
_____
_____
_____

1.45 The important point to note is that ac-

cording   to   the   _____   empirical law,
_____ of _____   effect
any event which _____ the   increases
_____ of a particular re-   probability
sponse in a given situation is a
_____.   reinforcer

1.46 Reinforcers are of two general types,
      _____ and _____.   positive, negative
      Either type, under the proper circum-
      stances, will _____ the prob-   increase
      ability of a _____.   response

1.47 The organism tends to _____   approach
      positive reinforcers and to _____   avoid
      negative reinforcers.   (escape)

CLASSIFICATION OF MOTIVES

Most motives may be classified into fairly broad categories on the basis of the particular components which constitute their motivational sequences. Of the numerous classification systems that have been suggested, only two currently more popular and perhaps more valid systems will be discussed here.

The first system classifies motives on the basis of their developmental backgrounds into two major types, *primary* and *secondary*. Primary motives, such as thirst and hunger, are based on the organism's *physio-chemical* processes and are basically unlearned. Secondary motives are not directly based on body chemistry and are generally thought to be *learned* through the organism's experience in its environment.

The second classification system is based on the *instrumental response* of the organism and classifies motives into approach or appetitive and avoidance or aversive drives. The goal of an approach motive, such as hunger, is referred to as a *positive* goal, that of an avoidance motive, such as pain, as a *negative* goal. It is important to note that in either case the organism's instrumental behavior (approach or avoidance) is directed toward reduction of the initiating drive.

1.48 Each motive can be defined in terms of
      the components of its motivational se-

quence. The hunger drive, for example, is aroused by food deprivation (need), initiates food seeking (instrumental behavior), and is reduced by food (the goal).

1.49 The fact that motives can be described in terms of their _____ _____ has led to the classification of motives in terms of these characteristics.

motivational
sequences

1.50 Upon studying the characteristics of motives, psychologists have arrived at numerous ways of c_____ them. Many of the older classifications have been abandoned, but *two* are now generally agreed upon.

classifying

1.51 The first of the _____ systems for _____ motives subdivides most drives into two types, *primary* and *secondary*. Primary drives are dependent on the organism's *physiochemical processes*.

two
classifying

1.52 Thirst is dependent on the physiochemical processes of the organism. Of the two types of drives in the first classification system, _____ and _____, thirst is, therefore, a _____ drive.

primary
secondary
primary

1.53 Since hunger is also a primary drive, we can say that it is principally based on the _____ _____ of the organism.

physiochemical
processes

1.54 Drives which are _____ as primary are also said to be unlearned.

classified

1.55 Hunger arises without any prior experience on the part of the organism. It is therefore a (primary, secondary) drive which is (learned, unlearned).

primary
unlearned

1.56 The principal characteristics of a primary drive are that it is _____ and is based on the organism's _____ _____.

unlearned
physiochemical
processes

1.57 Any drive which arises without previous learning is a _____ drive and represents one of the two types of _____ under the first classification system for motives.

primary

drive (motive)

1.58 The second type of drive in this classification system is called a se_____ drive. It is dependent on the individual experiences of the organism and is therefore basically different from the _____ drive.

secondary

primary

1.59 The strong desire of a college student to become an engineer is based primarily on the student's past experience and teaching. This striving is therefore an example of a _____ motive. Unlike a primary _____, it is _____.

secondary
motive (drive)
learned

1.60 Since a _____ motive is learned, we can conclude that it is not *ordinarily* based on the _____ _____ of the organism. For this reason, secondary motives are often referred to as *nonphysiological* drives.

secondary

physiochemical
processes

1.61 Most human beings are motivated by a desire to associate with others. This is another example of a nonphysiological

learning

drive based on _____.

nonphysiological

1.62 Secondary motives are called _____ motives because they are not usually directly based on the organism's biological needs.

1.63 There are a few exceptions to the general rule that secondary drives are nonphysiological. The individual who becomes addicted to heroin develops a *physiological* need for the drug. The drive is secondary

learned

in that it is _____, but it does have a physiological basis. If we keep this and related exceptions in mind, the primary-secondary classification system is a useful one.

1.64 The principal characteristics of a secon-

learned
nonphysiological

dary motive are that it is _____ and that it is usually _____. We shall discuss primary and secondary motives in greater detail in later chapters.

1.64a Beside each of the following characteristics, write "primary" or "secondary" to indicate which type of drive the characteristic best describes.

(1) secondary

(1) Based on experience _____

(2) Aroused by a physio-

(2) primary

logical need _____

(3) Aroused by electric-

(3) primary

shock stimulation _____

(4) secondary
(5) primary

(4) Acquired after birth _____
(5) Unlearned _____

1.65 The second classification system for

motives which we shall consider also subdivides most motives into two types, using
terms which describe the organism's
instrumental response relative to the *goal*
of the motive.

1.66 The two types of motives in this system
are *approach* or *appetitive* drives and
avoidance or *aversive* drives. When an
approach motive is aroused, the organism's instrumental response will be to
move toward the _____.   goal

1.67 When a rat deprived of food is placed
in a T-maze,

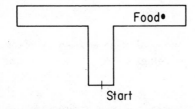

with food in the right arm of the maze,
the rat will learn to turn right and thus
(approach, avoid) the goal. Hunger is   approach
therefore classified as an _____   approach
or _____ motive.   appetitive

1.68 When the organism's _____   instrumental
_____ is to approach a goal,   response
the goal is called a *positive goal*.

1.69 Since the food-deprived rat approaches
food in the maze, the food can be said
to be a _____ _____.   positive goal

1.70 If the organism's instrumental response
carries it away from the goal, the motive

avoidance,
aversive

avoidance, aversive

is classified as an _____ or
_____ motive. If the rat is
stimulated with electric shock, it will attempt to avoid or escape from the
shock. It is therefore exhibiting an
_____ or _____
motive.

instrumental
response
negative goal

1.71 Since the rat's _____ _____
is to move away from the shock, the shock
is called a _____ _____.

avoid (escape)

avoidance
(aversive) motive

1.72 A *negative goal* is any goal which the
organism attempts to _____.
The child who runs because he fears that
his father will punish him is exhibiting
an aroused _____ _____.

negative

1.73 The goal of an aroused avoidance motive
is called a _____ goal.

avoidance
(aversive) motive
(drive)

1.74 If we are told that an animal's instrumental behavior is directed in relation to
a negative goal, we may conclude that
the action is the result of an aroused
_____ _____.

aversive
(avoidance)
antecedent
(stimulus)

1.75 If a rat is placed on a grid which is then
electrified, the rat will run off the
grid into an adjoining unelectrified
compartment. The rat is exhibiting an
_____ motive to the shock,
which is the _____ condition
for the arousal of the motive.

instrumental
reduction

1.76 In this situation the rat's action (running)
is called _____ behavior and
results in drive _____.

1.77 We have briefly considered two systems for classifying motives. In the first system, motives are subdivided into _____ and _____. In the second system, the two types of motive are _____ and _____.

primary, secondary
approach
   (appetitive)
avoidance
   (aversive)

1.78 It is easy to see, of course, that a given motive can be classified in either of the two systems or in both. Thus, hunger is a *primary approach* motive, since it has characteristics of both primary motives and approach motives.

1.79 Since a given motive can be _____ in both systems, the two systems are *independent*. That is, classification of a motive in one system does not determine or preclude its classification in the other.

classified

1.79a Each of the following is related to some aspect of the motivational sequence. Classify each as primary or secondary and as approach or avoidance.

(1) Hunger

_____ ; _____

(2) Escape from shock

_____ ; _____

(3) Desire for money

_____ ; _____

(4) Seeking food

_____ ; _____

(5) An embarrassing situation

_____ ; _____

(6) Thirst

_____ ; _____

(1) primary;
    approach
(2) primary;
    avoidance
(3) secondary;
    approach
(4) primary;
    approach
(5) secondary;
    avoidance
(6) primary;
    approach

(7) secondary;
    avoidance
(8) secondary;
    approach

(7) Working hard in order not to fail

_____; _____

(8) Desire to become a doctor

_____; _____

secondary
approach
  (appetitive)

1.80 The fact that the desire to become an engineer is classified in the first system as a _____ drive does not influence its classification in the second system as an _____ motive.

independent

1.81 The statement that desire for an engineering degree can be classified as a secondary approach motive supports the position that the two classification systems described are _____.

1.82 In concluding our discussion of motive classification, we should note that not all motives can be clearly classified in either or both of the systems described. The reason for this usually lies in an _incomplete knowledge_ of certain characteristics of the motive.

incomplete

1.83 Curiosity about the environment has been shown to have many of the characteristics of a drive. Its classification, however, is still in question, since we thus far have an _____ knowledge of its basis.

1.84 We have now had a brief introduction to some of the major concepts in motivation. The next chapters of the book will deal in some detail with primary and secondary motivation. Later we shall consider some of the major theoretical positions currently held and note some trends in the psychology of motivation.

PRIMARY DRIVES 2

As was noted previously, primary drives are physiologically based, unlearned motives. It is thought that most primary drives represent a general tendency of the body to maintain *equilibrium* among the internal physiological conditions of the body. This tendency is called *homeostasis,* a term originated by W. B. Cannon (1932).

Deviations from equilibrium may be caused by such conditions as lack of food or water or by sickness which elevates body temperature. The operation of hunger and thirst drives will be discussed in detail in Chapters 3 and 4. In the case of elevated temperature, the homeostatic mechanisms of the body are activated to reduce temperature. Thus, sweat glands and blood vessels dilate to allow cooling of the body.

2.1 We have said that the primary drives have   physiological
a _____ basis in the organism.   (physiochemical)
Actually, some psychologists have found
it convenient to subdivide primary drives
into *physiological drives* and *stimulation
drives.*

2.2 In general, *physiological* drives are those which are known to have a definite physiological or *physiochemical* basis, as we noted earlier. The basis for stimulation drives is not yet clear, although most psychologists agree that such drives are unlearned. We shall discuss here only the physiological drives.

primary

2.3 In order to understand the operation of most drives in the physiological subdivision of the _____ drives, it is necessary to study the concept of *homeostasis*, a term coined by the famous physiologist, W. B. Cannon (1932).

physiological

2.4 *Homeostasis*, which is essential to many ph_____ drives, may be defined as the tendency of the body to maintain a state of *equilibrium* among the internal physiological conditions of the body and to return to this equilibrium whenever the balance is disturbed.

2.5 If body temperature rises above the normal 98.6°F, various mechanisms in the body are activated in an attempt to bring the temperature back to normal. This attempt by the body to maintain equilibrium is

homeostasis

called _____.

motive (drive)

2.6 Whenever a physiological *need* arises, it activates a _____, and the *homeostatic* mechanisms of the body attempt to reduce this drive and thus return

equilibrium

the body to _____.

equilibrium

2.7 The mechanism of *homeostasis* in maintaining _____ has often been analogized to the *thermostat*, which can be set to maintain a constant temperature.

2.8 The maintenance of normal temperature is accomplished through the _____ mechanisms, which always tend to maintain internal _____ in the body.

homeostatic
equilibrium
(balance)

2.9 Because physiological drives activate homeostasis, they are often called _____ drives.

homeostatic

2.10 Temperature maintenance is an example of a physiological or _____ drive. When temperature rises above normal, the sweat glands are activated, and the evaporation of sweat from the body surface cools the body. At the same time, *dilation* (widening) of blood vessels brings blood to the surface of the body where it loses heat.

homeostatic

2.11 The _____ mechanisms of temperature control also work to warm the body when temperature drops. Muscle activity and tension increase, causing *shivering* and consequent heat production. Body *metabolism* may also increase somewhat.

homeostatic

THE AUTONOMIC NERVOUS SYSTEM

The principal mechanism of homeostatic control is the *autonomic nervous system* (ANS). This system consists of two branches, the sympathetic and the parasympathetic. The former tends to *expend* bodily energies and is often referred to as the *emergency* system, since it is maximally dominant during times of emergency. The parasympathetic system tends to *conserve* energy and is relatively dominant when the organism is at rest.

Closely associated with ANS in homeostatic control is the body's system of ductless glands, the *endocrine* system. This system, activated by the ANS, is dominated by the *pituitary* gland, which secretes hormones with widespread effects throughout the body.

dilation

2.12 The secretion by the sweat glands and _____ of blood vessels which lower body temperature are under the control of the *autonomic nervous system,* the principal mechanism of homeostatic control.

equilibrium
(homeostasis)

2.13 The *autonomic nervous system* consists of two branches, the *sympathetic* branch and the *parasympathetic* branch, each of which has fibers extending to the smooth muscles and glands of the body. Both work to maintain _____ in the body.

autonomic

2.14 The *sympathetic* subdivision of the _____ nervous system is often called the *emergency* system, since it responds during emergencies or rapid environmental changes.

sympathetic

2.15 This *emergency* or (sympathetic, parasympathetic) nervous system tends also to react as a whole. Thus, in fear or anger the heart rate and blood pressure *increase,* blood goes to the exterior musculature, and digestion slows.

sympathetic,
parasympathetic

increase

parasympathetic

2.16 The _____ and _____ branches of the autonomic nervous system generally produce *opposite* reactions. For example, while the action of the sympathetic system is to _____ blood pressure and heart rate, that of the _____ system is to *decrease* them.

2.17 In general, we may say that the sympathetic system tends to *expend* bodily energies in _____, while the parasympathetic *tends* to *conserve* energy when the organism relaxes.

emergencies

2.18 When a child is frightened by a barking dog, his immediate reactions are principally a function of the _____ system. When he goes to bed at night and relaxes, the _____ system is in control.

sympathetic

parasympathetic

2.19 The _____ and _____ divisions of the _____ nervous system constitute the principal mechanisms of _____.

sympathetic,
    parasympathetic
autonomic
homeostasis

2.20 Closely allied with both the parasympathetic system, which tends to _____ energy, and the sympathetic system, which _____ energy, is the *endocrine* system.

conserve
expends

2.21 The *endocrine* system consists of all the glands of the body which do not have ducts but rather secrete directly into the bloodstream and lymphatic systems. Endocrine glands are therefore called *ductless* glands.

2.22 These *ductless* glands, which are activated by the _____ nervous system, secrete chemicals known as *hormones*.

autonomic

2.23 One of the ductless or _____ glands, the *pituitary*, secretes several different _____ which exert extensive control over the body.

endocrine

hormones

2.24 The hormones secreted by the pituitary control bodily growth as well as the functioning of several other glands, including the gonads (sex glands), the thyroid, and the adrenal cortex. We will discuss the pituitary in more detail in connection with the thirst and sex drives.

ductless
  (endocrine)

2.25 Because of its extensive influence on other glands, the pituitary, a _____ gland, is sometimes called the *master gland*.

homeostasis
autonomic
  nervous system
endocrine

2.26 The maintenance of body equilibrium through _____ is controlled by the _____ _____ _____ and the _____ system.

sympathetic
parasympathetic
sympathetic

parasympathetic

2.27 The autonomic system consists of two subdivisions, the _____ system and the _____ system. In emergencies, the _____ system is in control. When the organism is at rest, the _____ is dominant.

pituitary
ductless

master gland

2.28 The _____ gland of the endocrine or _____ system exerts considerable control over the other glands. It is often called the _____ _____.

REGULATORY BEHAVIOR

2.29 Mention should also be made of an important factor which supplements physiological mechanisms in the maintenance of homeostasis. This factor is *regulatory behavior*, so named because it aids in the regulation of physiological conditions of the body.

2.30 Recalling the third step in the motivational sequence, we can say that *regulatory behavior* (Richter, 1943) is i_____ behavior which aids in reducing physiological drives.

instrumental

2.31 When a man suddenly becomes cold, muscle tension will increase and he will shiver. He may also put on a sweater or coat. Since his behavior has the effect of helping to reduce the drive (coldness), it may be called _____ behavior.

regulatory

2.32 Regulatory behavior is any behavior which helps to maintain balance or _____ among internal physiological states and thus aids in the process of _____.

equilibrium

homeostasis

2.33 We should conclude our discussion of homeostasis by noting some *exceptions* to the general rules. The first of these is that under certain conditions homeostasis may *fail*. The high fever which may accompany infection is an example of a little-understood breakdown of the homeostatic mechanisms controlling body temperature.

2.34 If a rat is deprived of food, the physiological need thus created arouses the hunger drive and the accompanying homeostatic mechanism and regulatory behavior. If, however, deprivation is continued beyond a certain point, the homeostatic drive ceases to increase and actually decreases. This is an example of the _____ of the homeostatic mechanism.

failure

2.35 A second consideration concerning homeostasis is that not all organic needs create _____ or physiological drives. The unfortunate individual who permits his car to operate in a closed garage may desperately need oxygen to replace the carbon monoxide which accumulates in his blood. He experiences no drive, however, and may die never knowing of his need.

homeostatic

2.36 Finally, it should be noted that *not* all physiological drives are homeostatic. The notable exception is the *sex drive*, which has not been shown to have any homeostatic basis. It is thus a physiological drive but not a _____ drive.

homeostatic

2.37 We must thus conclude that there are at least three limitations which should be placed on the concept of homeostasis: (1) In some instances the homeostatic mechanisms may _____; (2) some physiological needs do not activate homeostatic _____; (3) some drives, like sex, are _____ but apparently not _____.

fail

drives
physiological
homeostatic

2.38 State the three limitations which must be placed on the concept of homeostasis.
(1) _____
(2) _____
(3) _____

Refer to
frame 2.37

HUNGER 3

One of the most basic and important drives motivating the behavior of organisms is the *hunger* drive. This *primary approach* motive is important because of the necessary energy supplied to the body by food. In the absence of a hunger drive and consequently of food, the organism would, of course, quickly deteriorate and die.

The basic need (i.e., food) and the major changes in body physiology accompanying the activation of the hunger drive have long been known. One of the principal correlates of hunger is *stomach contraction,* and this has been shown to be associated with subjectively felt hunger *pangs.* At one time it was suggested that contractions were the principal and perhaps the only body changes caused by food deprivation and, hence, that hunger was a relatively simple motive.

However, subsequent studies showed that such was not the case. It was shown that hunger sensations (pangs) were accompanied not only by stomach contractions but also by complex changes in body physiology. Most of these changes are changes in the physiochemistry of the blood. It is now thought that these *chemical factors* are more important aspects of the hunger drive than are the accompanying stomach contractions. Some studies have shown, in fact, that although stomach contractions are not essential to the occurrence of hunger sensations, certain changes in blood chemistry are.

3.1 Hunger is one of the most important of the physiological drives, and, unlike sex, it is a _____ drive.

homeostatic

3.2 The primary importance of hunger lies in the fact that energy for the maintenance and functioning of the body must come from the metabolism of food. If an individual failed to eat for a long period of time because he had no _____ drive, he would, of course, die.

hunger

3.3 It has long been thought that *stomach contractions* are a major factor in the hunger drive. When an individual is in need of food, he can often feel these contractions and the (hunger pangs, metabolic changes) which accompany them.

hunger pangs

3.4 In a famous experiment (Cannon, 1934), subjects each swallowed a rubber balloon, which was then inflated. A recording pen attached to a tube from the balloon then marked a moving tape each time a stomach _____ squeezed the balloon. The subject also pressed a telegraph key each time he felt a hunger pang. It was found that the hunger pangs and stomach contractions occurred at the same time.

contraction

3.5 The Cannon (1934) experiment showed that there was a definite relationship between _____ _____ and stomach contractions. Thus, when you feel a hunger pang, it is probably pre-

hunger pangs

ceded and perhaps caused by a _____ _____.

stomach contraction

3.6 Unfortunately, the operation of the hunger drive is not so simple as it might initially appear. Tsang (1938) found that rats with their stomachs removed exhibited a hunger drive, ate, and learned like normal rats, even though they could not have stomach _____.

contractions

3.7 The Tsang (1938) experiment demonstrated that, in rats at least, _____ _____ were not necessary for the activation of the hunger drive.

stomach contractions

3.8 More recent evidence indicates that the most important factor in hunger may be *blood chemistry*. In fact, both stomach contractions and the accompanying sensations or _____ _____ are probably due to *chemical factors*.

hunger pangs

3.9 In one experiment blood transfused from a starving to a satiated dog caused stomach contractions in the satiated dog (Luckhardt and Carlson, 1915). This result suggests the importance of _____ factors in hunger.

chemical

3.10 Although the chemical factors in hunger are still not completely understood, most evidence indicates that *blood-sugar level* is of prime importance. For example, dextrose, which increases blood-sugar level, stops hunger contractions, while insulin, which decreases the level, induces contractions (Quigley, Johnson, and Soloman, 1929). This experiment provides evidence that stomach contractions are at

chemical

least in part dependent on _____ factors.

3.11 That human patients with their entire stomachs removed experience sensations of hunger (Wangensteen and Carlson, 1931) indicates that _____ _____ are not necessary for the hunger drive but do not preclude the necessity of _____ action.

stomach
contractions

chemical

3.12 We can say that hunger pangs are accompanied by _____ _____, which are probably primarily under the influence of _____ _____.

stomach
contractions

chemical factors

3.13 One chemical factor which is of importance in hunger is the organism's _____ - _____ level.

blood-sugar

3.13a State briefly the findings of the Cannon (1934) experiment. (See frame 3.5.)

There is a
definite rela-
tionship between
hunger pangs
and stomach
contractions.

_____
_____
_____
_____

Stomach contrac-
tions are not
necessary for
the activation
of the hunger
drive, at least
in rats.

3.13b State the findings of the Tsang (1938) experiment. (See frame 3.7.)

_____
_____
_____
_____

SPECIFIC HUNGERS

Like most primary drives, hunger is a *homeostatic* motive. The striving for equilibrium characteristic of all homeostatic drives is clearly seen in the phenomenon of *specific hungers*. When the organism is deprived of a particular substance, such as fat or salt, which is critical to its existence, the organism develops a desire for that substance. These desires for particular substances are appropriately called *specific hungers*.

Despite the existence of specific hungers, diseases known to result from dietary deficiencies do occur. There appear to be three primary reasons for these diseases. First, environmental and cultural influences forced upon the individual may result in certain deficiencies. Secondly, some food needs, such as vitamin A, do not produce specific hungers. Finally, the organism learns to prefer certain foods. These learned preferences, called *appetites,* may override specific deficiencies and cause the organism to remain deficient in necessary substances.

3.14　The *homeostatic* basis of hunger is clearly demonstrated in the phenomenon of *specific hungers.* Some Australian aborigines, for example, live principally on small animals which have an inadequate amount of fat. The aborigines' craving for fat sometimes becomes so great that they resort to cannibalism (Wilkins, 1929).

3.15　The forced cannibalism of the aborigines illustrates the general principle behind s_____ h_____,　　specific hungers namely, that these intense desires for specific substances result from a deficiency of these substances and a consequent need for them.

3.16　During pregnancy, some women crave somewhat unusual foods. In most instances these desires are examples of specific hungers arising from a _____　　deficiency of minerals, proteins, and fats.

3.17　In an experimental demonstration of the need basis of specific hungers, Richter (1936) found that rats increased their

chemical

blood-sugar
level

specific hungers

needs
(deficiencies)

needs
(deficiencies)

salt consumption after their adrenal glands were excised (causing them to lose salt). Like the hunger drive itself, specific hungers are based on _____ factors.

3.17a State one important chemical factor in hunger. _____

3.18 One of the most convincing demonstrations of the organism's ability to satisfy its needs and maintain homeostasis was the "cafeteria feeding" experiment of Davis (1928) in which human infants were allowed to select their own diets for periods ranging from six months to $4\frac{1}{2}$ years. The babies selected their diets so well that they surpassed normally fed children in growth. They were undoubtedly able to select such adequate diets only because of _____ _____.

3.19 The specific hungers of the infants in Davis's (1928) experiment were due to the presence of particular _____. The tendency to select foods that satisfy _____ is seen also in lower animals (Young, 1933).

3.20 If the tendency to select appropriate foods is so prevalent, why do dietary deficiencies exist in human beings? There are several reasons. The first may be called environmental and cultural influences. Beriberi, a disease caused by a deficiency of thiamine in the diet, is common in the Orient where polished rice containing no thiamine constitutes a substantial proportion of the diet.

3.21 The second reason is that some food
      needs do not produce a specific drive;
      i.e., they do not cause _____   specific
      _____. Rats deprived of vita-   hungers
      min A, for example, do not select food
      containing this vitamin (Wilder, 1937).

3.22 The final reason is *appetite:* the organism
      may *learn* to like foods that are of no
      value to him. Rats have been shown to
      learn responses rewarded by saccharin,
      which has no nutritive value to the animal
      (Sheffield and Roby, 1950).

3.22*a* State the three reasons (in any order)
      why dietary deficiencies may not cause
      specific hungers.   (1) environmental
      (1) _____   (2) no drive
      (2) _____   produced
      (3) _____   (3) appetite

3.23 Human beings who eat candy and cake
      to the exclusion of necessary vitamins
      are demonstrating the dominance of
      _____ over needs.   appetite

3.24 The basis for specific hungers is primarily
      chemical, while that for appetite is
      _____.   learning

3.25 Specific hungers cause the organism
      to select foods on the basis of
      the organism's _____, while   needs
      _____ causes selection of foods   appetite
      on the basis of learned desires.

3.26 We may conclude that hunger is
      basically a p_____ drive but   physiological
      that it may be modified or directed by
      _____.   learning

Thirst 4

In some respects, explanations for the activation of the *thirst* drive have paralleled those for the hunger drive. The *local* theory of thirst, stated by W. B. Cannon (1934), held that the need for water and consequent activation of the thirst drive result from local dryness of mucous membranes of the throat and mouth.

The parsimonious local theory, like the stomach contraction hypothesis for hunger, proved to be incomplete. Studies subsequent to Cannon's early work showed that it is not local dryness but general bodily dehydration that is one critical factor in thirst arousal. Other experiments have shown that water must reach the *bloodstream,* not merely the stomach, in order to effectively reduce thirst. This finding, of course, led to the hypothesis that changes in blood chemistry are as important in thirst as they are in hunger.

The blood-chemistry hypothesis, however, proved to be a false lead in the case of thirst. Instead, it was shown that the amount of water in body *cells* is probably the most important and basic aspect of thirst arousal. It is thus *cellular dehydration* that actually activates the thirst drive.

4.1 A drive which is even more critical to the survival of the organism than hunger is *thirst*. Like hunger, thirst is thus a _____ drive.

primary
(physiological)

4.2 When a person or an animal is deprived of water for a period of time, he will drink to alleviate his thirst _____. One early explanation for this behavior was a *local theory* of thirst.

drive

4.3 According to the *local theory* of W. B. Cannon (1934), the thirst drive, which is aroused by a _____ for water, is activated by local *dryness* of the mucous membranes of the mouth and throat.

need

4.4 More specifically, a reduced amount of body water reduces the amount of saliva secreted, and the resultant _____ of the mouth and throat activates the _____ _____.

dryness
thirst
drive

4.5 The extreme example of this mechanism would be that of the unfortunate individual lost in the desert. His intense drive for water would, according to the _____ theory, be a direct result of the painful _____ of his mucous membranes.

local
dryness

4.6 As stomach contractions are not the sole factor in hunger, so also is membrane _____ not the only factor in _____. In fact, dogs without salivary glands do not drink excessive amounts of water (Montgomery, 1931).

dryness
thirst

local

4.7 The fact that a man without salivary glands (and consequently a constantly dry mouth) also drank only a normal amount of water (Steggerda, 1941) is further evidence against the _____ theory.

salivary

4.8 Although dogs and human beings without _____ glands do not drink excessively, dryness is normally a reliable *indicator* of the *need* for water when it is directly related to *dehydration* throughout the body.

dehydration

4.9 The injection of hypertonic saline (salt) solution into human beings reduces or completely stops salivary flow, resulting in dryness of the mouth and excessive thirst. It is not, however, the local dryness but a more general reduction of body water or _____ which causes thirst (Holmes and Gregersen, 1947).

indicator
dehydration

4.10 In the salt-injection experiment, mouth dryness is simply an _____ of thirst. The important factor, _____, determines not only whether or not the the animal will be thirsty but also the *amount* it will drink.

4.10a State the local theory of thirst.

Thirst is due to a
 local dryness of
 the mucous
 membranes of
 the mouth
 and throat.

_____
_____
_____
_____
_____
_____
_____

4.10b Cite evidence against the local theory.

_____

_____

_____

_____

_____

_____

_____

The fact that a man without salivary glands also drank only a normal amount of water is evidence against the local theory.

4.11 Using weight taken after deprivation and after drinking as a measure of water deficit, Adolph (1941) found that dogs drank almost exactly the amount of water needed after deprivation. This is an example of the regulation of _____ of water intake by dehydration.

amount

4.12 It has also been demonstrated that the regulating factor is *not* the amount of water *taken into the stomach*. In some experiments the esophagus (tube between mouth and stomach) of dogs has been cut and the ends brought out through the skin (Adolph, 1941; Bellows, 1939). Although the water these dogs drank never reached the _____, they drank only the *amount needed to replace their deficit*.

stomach

4.13 The experiments described above have demonstrated that neither _____ of the mucous membranes nor water in the _____ is a primary factor in the regulation of the _____ drive.

dryness

stomach
thirst

4.14 A further finding of the Adolph (1941)

experiment was that if water was injected directly into the stomach, the dog did not immediately stop drinking. If forced to wait fifteen minutes before drinking, however, the dog consumed no water at all. Thus, water had to reach the *bloodstream* in order to reduce the thirst drive. Merely

stomach

putting water in the _____ had no effect.

bloodstream

4.15 Although Adolph (1941) demonstrated that water must reach the _____ to reduce thirst, he did not show that changes in *blood composition per se* were important.

blood

4.16 Other experiments have also failed to attribute any specific importance to _____ composition in thirst regulation. Rather, it appears that the amount of water in body *cells* is the determining factor.

thirst drive

4.17 The need for water and the consequent _____ _____ are probably primarily due to loss of water from body *cells* or *cellular dehydration*.

NEURAL MECHANISMS OF THIRST

It is now thought that the mechanism through which cellular dehydration activates the thirst drive is neural. Dehydration affects certain tissues, called *osmoreceptors,* which are located at the base of the brain. These special receptors in turn activate the *pituitary gland* and/or the *hypothalamus.* The pituitary, discussed in an earlier chapter, secretes the *antidiuretic hormone,* which functions to inhibit the elimination of urine and consequently to reduce thirst.

The importance of the antidiuretic hormone is seen when the posterior pituitary which produces it is damaged, stopping production of the hormone. The result is a serious condition known as *diabetes insipidus,* symptoms of which include excessive urination and intense thirst.

The hypothalamus, mentioned above, is an extremely important brain center which serves numerous functions related to motivation and emotion. Its exact function in thirst is not entirely clear. However, it has been shown that stimulation of or damage to the hypothalamus may affect the thirst drive.

4.18   When the body loses water, the resultant cellular _____ is thought to affect certain tissues at the base of the brain known as *osmoreceptors.*

        dehydration

4.18a State four hypotheses which have attempted to explain the operation of the thirst drive.
(1) _____
(2) _____
(3) _____
(4) _____

    (1) local theory
    (2) general
        dehydration
    (3) blood
        composition
    (4) cellular
        dehydration

4.19   The stimulation of the *osmoreceptors* which results from _____ _____ in turn causes stimulation of the *pituitary gland* and/or the hypothalamus.

        cellular
        dehydration

4.20   The posterior lobe of the *pituitary gland* secretes the *antidiuretic hormone,* which is known to be of primary importance in the regulation of water balance. Activation of the pituitary may be by an impulse from the _____.

        osmoreceptors

4.21   The *antidiuretic hormone,* which is secreted by the _____ gland, serves to *inhibit the elimination of urine* and consequently to reduce thirst.

        pituitary

40

4.22 If the posterior pituitary is damaged, stopping production of the _____ _____, the resultant condition is known as *diabetes insipidus*.

antidiuretic
hormone

4.23 The symptoms of *diabetes insipidus* include excessive urination and intense thirst. These symptoms are due to a lack of the _____ _____.

antidiuretic
hormone

4.24 In the normal animal or human being, water deprivation will cause c_____ d_____, which will cause stimulation of the sensitive _____ at the base of the brain.

cellular
dehydration

osmoreceptors

4.25 It is thought the osmoreceptors stimulate the posterior lobe of the _____ _____, which secretes the _____ _____ important in maintaining _____ balance.

pituitary gland
antidiuretic
hormone
water

4.26 We noted previously that the hypothalamus might also receive impulses from the _____. The hypothalamus is a small area in the brain which is of great importance in the regulation of thirst and other drives. We will consider its function in some detail in a later chapter.

osmoreceptors

4.26a Review briefly the process through which cellular dehydration serves as a "trigger" in the maintenance of water balance.

_____

_____

_____

Refer to pages
38 and 39.

APPETITE

Specific thirsts analogous to specific hungers apparently do not exist. Instead, the physiological basis for all thirst is the need for water. Acquired (learned) appetites do, however, exist, and these account for preference for certain beverages.

The learning of specific appetites may be based on any of several attributes of the preferred beverages. The beverage may have *narcotic* or *stimulating* properties. The preference may, on the other hand, be based on the *taste* or *social value* of the beverage. In any case, the specific preference is based on a learned appetite, not on a specific need.

4.27 Before leaving thirst, we should note that an animal with a specific deficiency (e.g., a need for carbohydrates) will select foods which alleviate the particular need. The physiological basis for all thirst, however, is the need for *water*. There are, therefore, no _____ _____ due to particular deficiencies.

specific thirsts

4.28 A general statement comparing hunger and thirst in this respect might be, then, that while a need for certain substances may produce _____ _____, thirst is physiologically based only on the need for _____, and there are therefore no physiologically _____ _____.

specific hungers

water

specific
  thirsts

4.29 If this is true, why do we sometimes experience a desire for coffee, a soft drink, or beer? The answer, of course, is acquired *appetites*. While the appetites are for particular beverages, the basic need underlying the thirst drive is that for _____.

water

appetites
(thirsts)

need

learn

appetite

learned
(acquired)

stimulating
taste

4.30 Specific _____ are acquired through *learning*. Because most beverages have a high percentage of water, the learned appetites still reduce the organism's basic _____.

4.31 The individual may _____ to desire a particular beverage because of its *stimulating* or *narcotic* properties, because of *taste*, or because of the *social value* of the beverage.

4.32 Coffee, for example, may be desired because of the *stimulating* properties of caffeine. Likewise, the individual may acquire an _____ for soft drink because of its taste.

4.33 Any one beverage may be desired for a combination of reasons. The young man may, for example, initially drink alcoholic beverages because of their *social value*. He may eventually, however, become an alcoholic, drinking them because of their *narcotic* properties.

4.34 If a beverage has narcotic properties, the individual may actually develop a *physiological need* for that beverage. Despite this fact, however, the appetite is still _____. It becomes a *physiological drive*, but is not one which is normally necessary for the survival of the organism.

4.35 Considering that tea, like coffee, contains caffeine, it is possible that an American college student who drinks tea may do so because of its _____ properties or because he likes the _____.

A Britisher on the other hand, may also drink it because of its _____ value.

social

4.36 Of the several bases for acquired appetites, it is probable that only beverages with _____ properties will produce acquired physiological drives.

narcotic

4.37 The reasons for particular acquired appetites include: _____ properties, _____ properties, _____, and _____ _____.

stimulating
narcotic
taste, social
value

4.38 An appetite for a given beverage may be acquired for one or a _____ of these reasons.

combination

4.39 It is important to note that most, if not all, beverages for which appetites are acquired will satisfy the basic need for _____, which is the basis of the _____ _____.

water
thirst drive

4.40 _____ of the mouth and lack of water in the _____ are not essential to the thirst drive. The most important single factor appears to be _____ _____.

Dryness
stomach

cellular
dehydration

SEX 5

The sex drive, like hunger and thirst, is a primary, physiological drive. Unlike other primary drives, however, it is not critical to the survival of the organism. To explain this discrepancy, some have argued that although sex is not necessary for individual survival, it is essential to species survival. In this sense, it is just as basic or "primary" as are hunger and thirst.

5.1 Like hunger and thirst, sex is basically a *physiological* drive which requires *instrumental* behavior for its reduction. Also, like other *primary* drives, the sex drive can be reduced by any of a number of different goals or incentives.

primary
physiological

5.2 Although the sex drive is _____ and _____, it differs from hunger and thirst in that it is not necessary for the *survival* of the individual organism. A man marooned on an island for several years will never die from the failure to reduce his sex drive. Should he run out of food or water, however, he will die in a very short time.

5.3 It has been argued that while the sex drive is not necessary for the survival of the _____, it is essential to the survival of the *species*.

organism
(individual)

5.4 If the sex drive were to suddenly become inactive in all dogs, the species would not _____ for very long. We can therefore say that sex is necessary for the continued existence of the _____.

survive

species

LOCAL STIMULATION

The activation of the sex drive is under the control of two factors, *local stimulation and hormonal balance.* The former, of little importance in lower animals, is critical in human beings. Stimulation of the penis in males or the clitoris in females is likely to arouse the sex drive and to heighten it before and during sexual intercourse. Other areas of the body, called erogenous zones, are also sensitive to stimulation. These areas include the lips, the nipples, and the female vagina.

5.5 The two principal physiological aspects of the sex drive are *local stimulation* and *hormonal control.* In *lower* animals, local stimulation is apparently not an essential component of the sex drive.

5.6 If the spinal cord is sectioned (cut), no sensations can be felt in the genitalia. The fact that sectioning the lower spinal cord in a male cat does not interfere with sexual behavior (Root and Bard, 1937) is evidence for the statement that stimulation in _____ animals is not essential to sexual behavior.

lower

5.7 In human beings, much the same situation prevails. Here, however, stimulation of the male *penis* or its female counterpart, the *clitoris*, is likely to arouse the sex drive and to heighten it before and during sexual intercourse. Thus, in human beings _____ _____ is an effective and sometimes essential aspect of the operation of the sex drive.

local stimulation

5.8 While the _____ in human females and the _____ in males are the primary areas for sexual stimulation, other areas of the body including the nipples, the lips, and the female vagina may be *erogenous* zones, arousing the _____ drive when stimulated.

clitoris
penis

sex

5.9 In human beings, _____ _____ or sexual arousal of _____ zones may be important in the activation and reduction of the sex drive. Without such stimulation, there is often no sharp reduction of the sex drive, or *orgasm*.

local
stimulation
erogenous

5.10 The failure to attain sexual drive reduction or _____ without _____ _____ is more often reported in females. The sex drive is generally both aroused and reduced more *gradually* in females than in males.

orgasm, local
stimulation

5.11 We have seen that local stimulation of _____ _____ is often important in both the activation and _____ of the sex drive, particularly in _____. As we shall see later, the individual's *culture*, *past learning*, and *experience* are also important.

erogenous zones

reduction
females

5.12 If the _____ _____ of
the human female are not stimulated, her
sex drive may not be _____.
Even if it is, she may not attain
_____ without further stimulation.

erogenous zones

activated
(aroused)
orgasm

5.13 The primary erogenous zones are the
male _____ and the female
_____. Other erogenous zones
include the _____ and _____
and the female _____.

penis
clitoris
lips, nipples
vagina

5.14 Thus far, we have said that _____
_____ is probably more im-
portant in human beings than in lower
animals. We shall now detail the influence
of _hormonal_ factors on the sex drive.

local
   stimulation

HORMONAL FACTORS

In lower animals, hormonal factors are more important than local
stimulation. The particular hormones involved in the sex drive are
produced in the _gonads_ and in the _pituitary gland_. The male gonads,
known as _testes,_ produce hormones called _androgens._ The female
gonads, or _ovaries,_ produce _estrogens._

Production of androgens and estrogens is activated by gonad-stimulating or _gonadotropic_ hormones. The latter are secreted by the
pituitary gland, which also controls the onset of puberty in both sexes.

5.15 Local stimulation and hormonal factors
constitute the two principal physiological
aspects of the sex drive. The hormones
important in sexual motivation are produced in two principal centers, the _gonads_
and the _pituitary gland_.

5.16 The male _gonads_ are known as testes,
those of the female as _ovaries_. Both
the testes and the ovaries secrete

hormones

_____ which are concerned with sex drive.

hormones
gonads

5.17 The _____ secreted by the male _____ or testes are *androgens*.

hormones

ovaries

5.18 The female sex _____ are called estrogens. They are secreted by the female gonads or _____.

testes
ovaries

hormone

5.19 Both the _____ of the male and the _____of the female are gonads. Each secretes a different _____.

androgens

estrogens

5.20 If the testes of the male are removed, _____ will no longer be secreted. If the female ovaries are removed, _____ will no longer be produced.

androgens,
estrogens

5.21 The action of the gonads in secreting _____ and _____ is governed by the *pituitary gland*.

Male: testes,
androgens
Female: ovaries,
estrogens

5.21a Give the specific names for male and female gonads and the sex hormones produced by each.
Male: _____
Female: _____

gonads

5.22 The *pituitary gland*, which governs the hormone production of the _____, secretes gonad-stimulating or *gonadotropic* hormones.

gonadotropic

androgens

5.23 If male gonads are not stimulated by the _____ hormones from the pituitary, they will not secrete _____.

5.24 Secretion of _____ by the female gonads or _____ also requires stimulation by _____ hormones from the _____ gland.

> estrogens
> ovaries
> gonadotropic
> pituitary

5.25 The onset of *puberty* in both sexes is also under the control of the pituitary. If the latter is excised (removed) before puberty, *adult* sexual characteristics do not develop (Ford and Beach, 1952).

5.26 We may see the importance of the pituitary gland in the sex drive in that it is responsible both for the stimulation of the _____ and for the onset of _____ and the consequent development of _____ sexual characteristics.

> gonads
> puberty
> adult

5.26a State briefly the relationship between the pituitary gland and the gonads.

_____

_____

_____

_____

> Gonadal secretion requires pituitary stimulation.

5.26b Match items in column (1) to those in column (2) by placing the proper letter in the blank preceding each item in column (2).

(1)	(2)	
(a) Male gonads	_____ orgasm	f
(b) Androgens	_____ erogenous	d
(c) Ovaries	_____ testes	a
(d) Clitoris	_____ pituitary	e
(e) Gonadotropic	_____ produced	b
(f) Drive	by testes	
reduction	_____ estrogens	c

The estrous cycle

Marked differences in sexual behavior are seen at different points in the evolutionary scale. In lower animals, such as rats, female sexual behavior is cyclical. The cycle, known as the *estrous cycle,* is completed once every four or five days in the white rat. At the height of the cycle, when ovulation occurs, the female is in heat or *estrus* and is maximally sexually receptive.

In infrahuman primates the *menstrual* cycle is closely analogous to the estrous cycle in rats. An important difference is that the female monkey may be sexually active when not in estrus, while the rat is active only at the time of ovulation.

Although the human female also has a menstrual cycle, sexual desire is relatively constant throughout the cycle. The exception is an increase in desire before and after menstruation. This increase, however, is probably due to anticipated and actual deprivation occurring at this time.

gonadotropic

5.27 In lower animals female sexual behavior is cyclical. The female white rat, for example, undergoes a complete *estrous cycle* about very four or five days. Each cycle is initiated by the _____ hormones from the pituitary gland.

estrous

5.28 The height of the sexual or _____ cycle is called heat or *estrus.* At this time *ovulation* occurs, and the female is maximally sexually *receptive.*

gonadotropic
pituitary

estrus

5.29 The _____ hormones secreted by the _____ gland initiate the estrous cycle in female rats. When ovulation occurs, the female is in heat or _____. It is at this time that estrogen production is maximal.

estrus

5.30 When the female rat is not in _____, she is not sexually receptive and will resist the advances of the male.

5.31 On the day of estrus or maximal sexual
_____, the female rat is also
extremely *active*. In fact, her activity level,
as measured by revolutions of a revolving
drum, is maximal at estrus (Stone, 1939).

receptivity

5.32 Gonadotropic hormones initiate the
_____ cycle. When ovulation
occurs, the female rat is in _____
and is sexually _____ and generally _____.

estrous
estrus
receptive
active

Sexual behavior in higher animals

5.33 As we go up the evolutionary scale, we
see a definite change in the pattern of
sexual receptivity. In infrahuman primates
(monkeys and chimpanzees) the *menstrual
cycle* is closely analogous to the estrous
cycle of the rat.

5.34 The monkey or chimpanzee, like the rat,
shows maximal sexual activity at the time
of ovulation when the animal is in
_____ (Yerkes and Elder, 1936).
At this time a maximal amount of the
hormone _____ is produced.

estrus

estrogen

5.35 The important difference between the rat
and the monkey is that in the latter females may also be sexually active when
not in estrus. The female is still, however,
more _____ at estrus when
_____ production is high.

receptive
estrogen

5.36 The cycle of sexual activity in the rat is
the _____ _____,

estrous cycle

menstrual cycle

that in the infrahuman primate the
_____ _____. The
human female also has a menstrual cycle.

5.37 The human female is largely emancipated
from the influence of hormones on sexual
behavior. Unlike the rat and the monkey,
she does not have a time of heat or

estrus

_____.

estrogen

5.38 As with the rat and monkey, the human
female has increased _____ production at the time of ovulation. Studies
have shown, however, that there is no increase in sexual desire at this time (Davis,
1929).

estrus

5.39 The human female does not experience
_____ at the time of ovulation.
Rather sexual desire remains constant
throughout the month except for a marked
increase *before and after menstruation.*

hormonal

5.40 The *constancy* of sexual desire in the human
female demonstrates her relative freedom
from _____ control. The in-
crease in desire before and after menstruation may be due to the anticipated and
actual *deprivation* occurring at this time.

deprivation
physiological
(hormonal)

5.41 If, as we have speculated, the increase in
sexual desire near menstruation is due to
_____, there may be little or
no _____ basis for this phenomenon.

5.42 As a general rule, we may state that as we
go up the evolutionary scale, there is pro-

gressively less hormonal control over sexual behavior. This is supported by the fact that the strength of the sex drive in human females is quite _____ through-out the month.

constant

5.43 Further support for the observation that the sex drive of lower animals is under _____ hormonal control than the sex drive of higher animals is found in observations of sexual behavior following *ovariectomy* (removal of the ovaries). In rats and monkeys there is no periodic estrus or increase in activity following ovariectomy. There is, in fact, a complete loss of sexual receptivity in females of these species (Beach, 1942).

greater

5.44 Human females experience no loss of sexual desire following ovariectomy (Clauberg and Schultze, 1934; Frank, 1929). This is quite different from the complete cessa-tion of _____ in rats and monkeys.

estrus
(desire)
(receptivity)

5.45 If estrogen is injected into an ovariecto-mized female rat or into a sexually imma-ture rat, the rat will become sexually responsive, and the cycle of sexual recep-tivity or the _____ cycle will return, although it may be somewhat irregular.

estrus

5.46 Monkeys without ovaries (i.e., _____ monkeys) also respond positively to estro-gen therapy. In this case, however, the menstrual cycle becomes quite regular, with the monkey receptive, as usual, at _____.

ovariectomized

estrus

5.47 The effect of injected female sex hormones,

estrogen

or _____, on human beings is not consistent. In some cases it fails completely, while in others positive effects are observed (Beach, 1947).

5.48 In general, then, we have three sets of facts in support of the contention that

less

there is _____ hormonal control of the female sex drive higher in the evolutionary scale than there is in the lower animals:

(1) Rats and monkeys are most receptive

estrus

constant

at _____, while human beings have a relatively _____ sex drive.

Ovariectomy

(2) _____ causes a greater and more rapid decrease in sex drive in lower animals than in human beings.

estrogen

(3) Injected _____ has a definite effect on lower animals, while its effect on human beings is inconsistent.

5.49 The sexual behavior of males of lower animal species is under *less hormonal control* than that of females. This is attested by the fact that *immature* male rats incapable of ejaculation will *mount* receptive females (Beach, 1947).

5.50 The fact that an experienced male rat will continue sexual activity for about six months after removal of the testes (Beach, 1947) is further evidence that the sex drive of the male of this species is under

hormonal

less _____ control than that of females.

5.51 The removal of the male gonads or

_____ is called *castration*, while the removal of female gonads is known as _____ .

testes

ovariectomy

5.52 If the testes of an experienced male rat are removed (i.e., he is _____), he will continue sexual activity for about _____ _____ . Normal mating behavior *never* develops if the male is castrated before *puberty*.

castrated

six months

5.53 As is the case with females, there is _____ hormonal control of male sexual behavior as we go up the evolutionary scale. Some dogs, for example, continue to copulate for two years after castration.

less

5.54 As we might expect, the sexual behavior of subhuman primates is only slightly affected by castration and that of human males is often not affected at all. This is evidence of decreased _____ _____ in higher animals.

hormonal
   control

5.55 When the male rat's testes are removed through _____ , what is the usual effect on his sexual behavior?

_____
_____
_____

castration
He will continue
   sexual activity
   for about
   six months.

5.56 The facts that dogs retain their sex drive for two years after castration and that monkeys are only slightly affected by castration is evidence of the progressive decrease in importance of _____ as we go up the evolutionary scale.

hormones

5.57 Studies employing *injected* sex hormones yield the expected results. Male hormones injected into castrated male guinea pigs (Seward, 1940) or rats (Stone, 1939) reinstate sexual behavior, while in man results are not at all clear.

THE EFFECTS OF LEARNING ON SEXUAL BEHAVIOR

As the importance of hormones decreases in higher animals, the importance of learning increases. In man, learning results in a variety of sexual *appetites*. The predominant cultural norm in our society dictates the learning of *heterosexual* preference. Some individuals, however, learn to prefer homosexual partners. Other, more specific sexual preferences may also be learned.

hormones

5.58 If the importance of _____ is decreased in higher animals, the importance of *learning* is greatly increased.

eliminates

learning

5.59 The observation that removal of the male gonads eventually _____ the sex drive in male rats but has little or no effect on human beings is evidence for the increased importance of _____ in the sexual behavior of the latter.

estrus

5.60 Male rats and dogs can successfully copulate with a female in heat or _____ on their first attempt. Male chimpanzees, however, must *learn* to copulate, often with the aid of an experienced female.

learning

learned

5.61 Because _____ is not necessary, the sexual behavior of rats is said to be *instinctive*. That of chimpanzees and human beings, on the other hand, is in large part _____.

5.62 Man's sex drive is often suppressed by the *mores* of his particular *society*. This social suppression of sexual behavior is further evidence of the importance of _____ in human sexual behavior.

learning

5.63 While the sexual behavior of rats is _____, that of man is greatly influenced by the _____ of his society. There are also, as in hunger and thirst, *learned* sexual *appetites* in man.

instinctive
mores

5.64 Most adults in our society are heterosexual; i.e., they prefer partners of the opposite sex. Some, however, deviate from this norm and prefer *homosexual* partners. In each case, the preference is a sexual a_____ which is _____.

appetite,
learned

5.65 In most societies, the _____ governing sexual behavior encourage *heterosexual* activities, since these are necessary for the *propagation* of the society.

mores

5.66 Individuals who prefer partners of the same sex are exhibiting _____ behavior and in so doing are deviating from the _____ of our society.

homosexual

mores

5.67 Both general types of human sexual behavior (i.e., _____ and _____) are examples of sexual _____ acquired through _____.

heterosexual,
homosexual
appetites,
learning

5.68 Other, more specific sexual appetites may also be _____. For example, different individuals prefer different positions for copulation.

learned

heterosexual

propagation

5.69 Most societies encourage _____ activities because these are essential to the _____ of the society.

5.70 Homosexuality is thought of as *abnormal* in our society because the social

mores,
  heterosexual

_____ call for _____ behavior.

5.71 In both males and females, the importance

hormones
learning

of _____ in sexual behavior decreases and that of _____ increases in the higher animals.

5.72 Sexual behavior which is controlled primarily by hormones, as in the rat, is said

instinctive

to be _____ behavior. We shall discuss this special type of behavior in more detail shortly.

5.73 Place the proper letter beside each of the following statements to indicate whether it is most likely to apply to: (a) the human being, (b) the monkey, or (c) the rat.

c
              _____ (1) Mostly unlearned sexual behavior

a
              _____ (2) Homosexuality

c
              _____ (3) Receptive only at estrus

b
              _____ (4) Most receptive at estrus; somewhat receptive at other times

a
              _____ (5) Most receptive just before and after menstruation

a
              _____ (6) Specific sexual appetites

PAIN DRIVE 6

The pain drive is classified as a primary avoidance motive, since the organism strives to avoid or escape from pain.

The mechanism of pain arousal is the stimulation of *free nerve endings* in the skin or organs of the body. Electric shock, for example, stimulates free nerve endings in the skin. These receptors relay the stimulation over nerve pathways to the spinal cord and brain, where the sensation of pain is experienced.

In the case of electric shock, *termination* of the shock is reinforcing, since shock termination following a particular response increases the probability of that response. Hence, as food is a positive reinforcer, shock termination is a negative reinforcer.

6.1 We have thus far discussed only approach or _____ drives. It was noted earlier, however, that there are also _____ drives, such as those reinforced by shock. Pain is such a drive.

appetitive

aversive
(avoidance)

6.2 While hunger, thirst, and sex are all

approach
  (appetitive)
avoidance
  (aversive)

_____ motives, pain is an _____ motive. If a rat receives shock in one compartment of a box, it will soon learn to *avoid* or *escape* that compartment.

pain

6.3 The shock received in the first compartment stimulates pain receptors in the skin and activates the p_____ drive. The receptors for pain are generally thought to be *free nerve endings*.

pain
avoidance
  (aversive)

6.4 When *free nerve endings* are stimulated by shock, a "normal" animal experiences a sensation of pain and the _____ drive, a primary _____ motive, is activated.

free

nerve

6.5 If the rat is in the compartment when shock stimulates the _____ _____ endings, it will learn to turn a wheel which opens a door into the unshocked compartment. This type of learning is called *escape* learning.

It is an
avoidance drive.

6.5a How does the pain drive differ from hunger and thirst?

_____

6.6 If the rat is given a *warning signal* or cue, such as a light, before shock comes on, it will learn to leave the compartment in response to the light. This is called *avoidance* learning. Both escape and avoidance are based on the

pain drive

_____ _____.

free nerve

6.7 The principal receptors for pain are _____ _____

_____. When these are stimu-
lated, the rat will learn to perform
tasks in order to _____ or
_____ the shock stimulus.

              endings

              avoid
              escape

6.7a Name the receptors for pain and the
two types of learning based on the pain
drive.

_____

_____

              free nerve
                endings
              escape
              avoidance

6.8   In discussing the hunger drive, it was
noted that food acts as a *positive reinforcer* of behavior which leads to reduction of the hunger drive. In the case of
the pain drive, it is the *termination
of shock* which is reinforcing, since
shock termination produces drive

_____.

              reduction

6.9   Since pain is an _____ drive,
and since shock _____ is reinforcing, shock is called a *negative reinforcer.*

              aversive
              termination

6.10 When the rat learns to leave the compartment in response to a warning signal before the shock is turned on, he has under-
gone _____ learning. In
leaving the compartment before shock
onset, it avoids the shock, which is a
_____ reinforcer.

              avoidance

              negative

6.11 In both _____ and _____
learning, the termination of a pain stimulus serves as a _____.

              avoidance,
                escape
              reinforcer

6.12 In the experiment we have been discussing, the pain is a primary _____

              aversive

62

negative
termination

drive, shock is a _____ reinforcer, and t_____ of shock
is the *goal* or *incentive*.

approach
  (appetitive)
hunger

6.13 We might compare this experiment with
one in which a food-deprived rat learns
to press a bar for food pellets. In this
case the primary _____ drive
is _____, and the incentive is
food, which is also a positive reinforcer.

primary
appetitive
  (approach)
aversive
  (avoidance)
positive,
  negative

6.14 Although both hunger and pain are
_____ drives, they differ in that
one is an _____ drive, while
the other is an _____ drive.
The reinforcers differ in that one is
_____, the other_____.

EFFECTS OF LEARNING AND PERCEPTION

6.15 Like the appetitive drives, the pain drive
can be influenced by *learning* and *perception*. A well-known example is the case of
World War II soldiers. Only one out of
three seriously wounded soldiers required
morphine to reduce pain, while four out
of five civilians with similar wounds needed
morphine. One explanation is that escape
from combat was reinforcing for the
soldiers, while the possibility of surgery
produced fear and enhanced pain in
civilians (Melzack, 1961).

6.16 Another example is that of individuals
actively engaged in sports, such as box-
ing. These men often sustain serious injury, but because their *attention* is con-
centrated on the sport, pain is not felt.

The above examples indicate that pain, although it is a _____ drive, can be influenced by learning and perception.

primary

6.17 Women in our society generally experience considerable pain in childbirth (if drugs are not used), while those in some other societies experience relatively little pain. The difference in perception is undoubtedly in great part due to the fact that girls in our culture are taught to expect pain in childbirth, while those in other cultures are not. This is an example of the influence of _____ on pain.

learning

6.17a In what important way are all four primary drives discussed the same?

_____

_____

_____

All have physiological bases but are influenced by learning.

6.18 Pain may also serve as a basis for the development of *secondary motives*, particularly *fear*.

THE DEVELOPMENT OF SECONDARY MOTIVES

Although pain is itself a primary drive, it may serve as the basis for the development of certain secondary motives, particularly fear. That fear is a secondary (learned) motive has been demonstrated in experiments in which an organism learns a new response through reinforcement by a previously neutral cue. Thus, when a neutral cue is paired with a pain-producing stimulus, the organism comes to exhibit a fear response to the previously neutral cue. Fear is thus a secondary motive based on the primary pain drive.

6.19 In an extension of the example cited previously, rats were shocked in a white compartment and allowed to escape by running to a black compartment. To show that a *fear* of the white compartment had developed, the rats were then given a series of nonshock trials, during which they learned to turn a wheel in order to escape from the now-enclosed white compartment (Miller, 1948). These findings indicate that fear is learned, since it is a response to the previously *neutral* cues of the white box, and that it is a d_____, since it motivated the learning of a new response (wheel turning).

drive (motive)

6.20 It can thus be seen that fear is an *acquired* or s_____ drive based on the _____ pain drive.

secondary
primary

6.21 Fear is said to be acquired because it is a response to previously neutral cues. It is a drive because it _____ the organism to _____ a new response.

motivates
learn

6.22 If neutral cues, such as the white box, which are associated with a primary drive come to elicit a response which can itself serve to motivate the organism, the latter is called a _____ drive. One example of such a drive is the _____ drive.

secondary
 (acquired)
fear

6.23 Acquired drives differ from primary drives in that the former are based on _____, while the latter are principally based on _____ processes. Secondary motives will be discussed in some detail in a later section.

learning
physiological

6.24 State the important implications of Miller's (1948) study.

_____
_____
_____
_____
_____
_____
_____
_____
_____
_____
_____

Miller's study indicated that fear is learned since it is a response to the previously neutral cues of the white box and that it is a drive since it motivated the learning of a new response (wheel turning).

INSTINCT 7

Instinct has been an important concept in the history of psychology. It originated with Stoic philosophers and has since had alternating periods of popularity and disfavor. A decline in popularity following its Stoic origin was reversed in the early twentieth century, when instinct became an important aspect of the theories of William James (1890), William McDougall (1926), and Sigmund Freud.

Despite its importance in the work of these prominent psychologists, instinct declined in popularity during the 1920s, when it was realized that there were numerous inconsistent definitions of the concept. It appears that many psychologists currently see a need for a concept like instinct, and its popularity is therefore now on the increase. Current usage of the term differs, however, from earlier usages in that instinct is now a carefully and quite consistently defined concept.

In the current definition, instinctive behavior has five specific characteristics. It is *complex, rigidly patterned, automatic, unlearned,* and *species-specific.* These characteristics will be explained in greater detail in the discussion which follows.

7.1   An important concept which we have

thus far only touched upon is that of *instinct*. We noted that the sexual behavior of the rat is primarily *instinctive* and implied that it is so called because of its unlearned nature. This, however, proves to be an inadequate definition of _____.

instinct

7.2 Historically, instinct is a concept of long standing, originating with the Stoic philosophers and having its early psychological history in the theories of William James (1890), William McDougall (1926), and (W. B. Cannon, Clark Hull, Sigmund Freud).

Sigmund Freud

7.3 Because of the great variation and inconsistency in the definitions and uses of the term, instinct, which had been important in the theories of Freud, James, and _____, declined in popularity in about 1920.

McDougall

7.4 Despite its decline in the 1920s which was primarily due to the variation and _____ in definitions of the term, instinct has now returned to psychology as a useful but *carefully defined* concept.

inconsistency

7.5 A major difference between the early use of instinct, as in the theories of _____, _____, and _____, and the current use of the term is that formerly there were numerous inconsistent definitions, while now instinct is a _____ defined concept.

James,
McDougall,
Freud

carefully

7.6 We have said that there have been four

important periods in the history of instinct.

(1) The early philosophical use of the
    term by the _____ philosophers

Stoic

(2) The early psychological theories of
    _____, _____,
    and _____

James, Freud,
McDougall

(3) The decline of the popularity of the
    instinct concept due to inconsistencies in the _____ of the term

definitions

(4) The current use of the term in
    which instinct is a _____
    _____ concept

carefully
defined

7.7 To aid in understanding a more specific definition of instinct, let us give a fairly detailed example of the instinctive courting behavior of the three-spined stickleback, a small European fish. The courting pattern begins in early spring, probably as a direct result of *hormones* discharged into the blood. The male first establishes an area or territory which he defends against invasion by all other fish. He next digs a pit in the sand and covers it with weeds to serve as a nest. With the completion of the nest, further hormonal changes cause the underside of the male to change color from a dull gray to bright red. When he now encounters a female whose body is swollen with eggs, he begins a dancing, zigzag movement. This movement and the red underside of the male serve as *critical stimuli* for sexual behavior in the female. She enters the nest and, when prodded by the male, lays her eggs, which he then fertilizes. When the male's mating urge is depleted, his color changes back to dull gray, and he fans the water over the nest to increase the supply of oxygen to the eggs. Importantly, if any step in the sequence is changed or blocked, the entire pattern is broken and no mating occurs (Tinbergen, 1952).

7.8   We can now define _____ behavior in terms of our example as having at least five specific characteristics. First, it is *complex*. This is quite obvious in the behavior of the stickleback described above, which involved a number of specific steps, each a complex behavioral pattern in itself.

instinctive

7.9   Secondly, instinctive behavior is *rigidly patterned*. Each step must occur before the following steps can take place. For example, the male stickleback will not seek a female until the nest is completed. This orderly sequence is probably at least in part due to the release of _____ into the blood.

hormones

7.10 Next, instinct is *automatic*. The behavior is elicited by specific *stimuli*. When these stimuli are presented, the behavior elicited varies only slightly or not at all, no matter what conditions prevail. Thus, the female seeing the red belly and zigzag dance of the male will always follow him to the nest. The red spot and dance serve as _____ for the female sexual behavior.

stimuli

7.11 In addition to being _____,

complex

patterned,
automatic

rigidly _____, and _____,
instinctive behavior is *unlearned*. It
requires no previous experience or observation on the part of either male
or female.

7.12 Finally, the behavior is *species-specific*.
All three-spined sticklebacks will follow
the exact mating sequence described
above. Other species, however, will follow different sequences. The fact that no
experience is needed for the behavior
pattern to emerge indicates that it is

unlearned

also _____.

(1) complex
(2) rigidly
       patterned
(3) automatic
(4) unlearned
(5) species

7.13 The defining characteristics of instinctive
behavior are that it is:

(1) _____
(2) _____
(3) _____
(4) _____
(5) _____ - specific

7.14 The fact that the female will spawn her
eggs in the nest when prodded by the
male indicates that the spawning behavior is automatic. The prodding is a

stimulus
instinctive
   (unlearned)
stickleback

_____ which releases the next
step in an _____ behavior pattern. The species in which the above
sequence occurs is the _____.

7.15 Instinctive behavior generally does not
involve a single, simple reaction but is

complex

rigidly
   patterned

rather quite _____, involving
a number of steps which occur in a
_____ _____ se-
quence.

7.16   Loggerhead turtles are hatched from eggs
       laid on the beach by the female turtle.
       The young loggerheads always head di-
       rectly toward the sea when hatched.
       This would indicate that this species
       _____ goes toward the ocean.   instinctively

7.17   To explain the automatic nature of
       _____ behavior, scientists use   instinctive
       the concept of the *innate releasing
       mechanism* (IRM). This refers simply to
       the fact that without previous experience
       the appropriate stimulus will release a
       particular behavior pattern.

7.18   One example of the IRM is found in
       newly hatched goslings. These birds will
       follow the first moving object they see in
       their environment. Normally, this would
       be the mother, but it has been found that
       they will follow a man, a cardboard cube,
       or almost any moving object in the en-
       vironment. This behavior is called *im-
       printing*. In this case the moving object
       is the _____ which releases an   stimulus
       instinctive behavioral pattern.

7.19   Some experiments (Hess, 1959) have
       shown that ducklings will follow a moving
       decoy wired to emit sounds. The behavior
       is referred to as _____. It may   imprinting
       be explained in terms of the innate   releasing
       _____ _____, for   mechanism
       which the decoy is a _____.   stimulus

7.20   The fact that the following behavior
       or _____ of young birds   imprinting
       arises without training exemplifies the

unlearned

_____ character of instinctive behavior. The fact that the birds will always or nearly always imprint to the first moving object in their environment demonstrates that instinctive behavior is

automatic

a_____.

7.21 The loggerhead turtles mentioned previously move toward the sea on moonlit nights. Since the ocean reflects more light than sand, it has been proposed that the turtles actually are going toward the more intense light. This is another example of behavior initiated by a specific

stimulus
releasing
 mechanism

_____. It can be explained in terms of the innate _____

_____.

7.22 The fact that the IRM has been used as an explanatory concept should not be taken to imply that the physiological basis of the mechanism is completely known—in fact, it is not. The concept is merely used as a possible explanation for the fact that instinctive patterns are

automatically
stimuli

a_____ released by specific

_____.

It is complex,
 rigidly pat-
 terned, auto-
 matic, unlearned,
 and species-
 specific.

7.23 State the five defining characteristics of instinctive behavior.

_____

_____

_____

_____

Without previous
 experience the
 appropriate
 stimulus will

7.23a Briefly define and give an example of IRM.

_____

_____

_____
_____
_____
_____
_____
_____
_____
_____

release a particular behavior pattern. An example of this might be the following of a moving object by goslings.

HEREDITY VERSUS ENVIRONMENT

7.24 Having defined instinct in terms of five characteristics, all of which imply the *hereditary* nature of instinctive behavior, we can now ask whether the *environment* and *experience* or *learning* of the organism can modify this behavior. The answer is, unequivocally, yes.

7.25 If an experienced male rat, whose sexual behavior is largely instinctive and under the control of hormones secreted by the gonads, is castrated, the animal will continue to engage in sexual behavior for some time thereafter. This would indicate that the sexual behavior of the rat has been influenced by _____.

experience (learning)

7.26 On moonless nights young loggerhead turtles will follow a beam of artificial light, even though it leads away from the ocean (Daniel and Smith, 1947). Thus, the i_____ sea-going behavior of the turtles can be modified by producing a change in their _____.

instinctive

environment

7.27 In discussing the sex drive, we noted that, as the human level of development is

learning

instinctive

approached, the influence of *hormones* on sexual behavior decreases and that of _____ increases. This constitutes another example of the modification of basically _____ behavior by environmental influences.

learning,
  (experience)
environment

7.28 It is not to be implied that instinctive behavior itself is learned or in any way deviates from the defining characteristics previously noted. Rather, instinctive behavior, which is unlearned, may be *modified* by the _____ and _____ of the organism.

INSTINCT IN HUMAN BEINGS

rigidly
  patterned
automatic,
  unlearned
species-specific

7.29 Are there behavioral patterns in human beings which conform to our definition of instinct as being complex, _____ _____, _____, _____, and _____ - _____? We have already noted that human sexual behavior does not conform to these criteria, since it is not at all stereotyped and is largely learned.

7.30 Human maternal behavior likewise does not appear to be instinctive, since it varies considerably from one society to another and since it must be learned. Further, studies have shown that most expectant mothers do not fully desire the coming child.

instinctive

7.31 The examples cited above indicate that human behavior is not _____. Perhaps the most general indication of this is the great variability and adaptability of human behavior.

7.32 Unlike lower animals, which must rely on rigidly patterned instinctive behavior for survival, human beings can react with any of a _____ of behaviors in a given situation.

variety
(number)

7.33 The two characteristics which most clearly establish the noninstinctive character of human behavior are its _____ and _____.

variability
adaptability

7.34 A rat forced into a corner by an adversary will show a characteristic pattern of aggressive behavior. A human being in the same situation, however, may attempt any of a variety of solutions, including verbalization. The behavior of the rat is primarily _____, while that of the human being is learned, as demonstrated by the fact that the human being can _____ his behavior to the situation.

instinctive

adapt

7.35 Behavior is generally not instinctive if it shows _____ and _____.

variability
adaptability

7.36 Human beings probably have (much, little or no) instinctive behavior.

little or no

Limbic System 8

In the preceding chapters, we have noted some of the physical and physiological concomitants of primary drives (e.g., blood-sugar level in hunger). While this peripheral physiology is important, one of the most significant influences on primary drives is that of certain areas of the brain.

One neural (brain) area of particular importance is the *limbic system*. This complex system consists, in part, of the *hypothalamus,* the *septal area* or *septum,* and the *amygdala*. These three areas have extensive influence over the activation, operation, and satiation of the primary drives.

The most influential area, the hypothalamus, has been studied primarily through the use of ablation (destruction) and stimulation of brain tissue. These techniques have revealed several specific areas within the hypothalamus which have particular types of influence. Two of these areas, the *central* area and the *lateral* area, are of importance in the hunger drive. Ablation of the central area increases appetite, while ablation of the lateral area decreases appetite. Stimulation of either of these areas produces an effect opposite to that produced by ablation. From this evidence, it has been hypothesized that the central area is the brain center which *inhibits* the hunger drive, while the adjacent lateral area is an *excitatory* center for hunger.

8.1   The primary drives, such as _____,   hunger
      _____, and _____, do   thirst, sex
      not operate entirely without influence
      from the brain. In fact, there are brain
      areas which appear to be critical in the
      arousal and satiation of these drives. The
      principal area with which we shall be con-
      cerned here is the *limbic system*.

8.2   The *limbic system*, which is important in
      the control of _____ drives, is   primary
      composed, in part, of three principal areas.
      These are the *hypothalamus*, the *septal
      area* or *septum*, and the *amygdala*.

8.3   Since hunger is a primary drive, it is
      under the influence of a brain area
      called the _____ system. This   limbic
      system includes the hypo_____,   hypothalamus
      the sep_____, and the   septum
      amyg_____.   amygdala

8.4   The *hypothalamus*, which is one part of
      the _____ system, is a small   limbic
      structure, perhaps the size of a kidney
      bean, which is located below the center
      of the brain, approximately above the roof
      of the mouth.

8.5   The septum, also a part of the
      _____ _____, is lo-   limbic system
      cated above and slightly in front of the
      hypothalamus.

8.6   A third part of this system, the
      _____, is located somewhat be-   amygdala
      low and behind the hypothalamus.

8.7 It should be noted that, like all brain structures, the areas of the limbic system are *paired*. That is, there is one hypothalamus on each side of the brain, one amygdala on each side, and one septum on each side.

hypothalamus
septum,
   amygdala

8.8 Taken together, the _____, the _____, and the _____ are three parts of the limbic system.

8.9 Of these structures the one most important in controlling primary drives is the hypothalamus. Its influence has been studied with two principal techniques, *ablation* (i.e., destruction) and *stimulation*.

8.10 Both ablation and stimulation of this area are generally (though not always) carried out by inserting fine bipolar electrodes into the brain. These are insulated except at the tip, which is located in the structure of interest. A low-intensity current passed through the electrode will stimulate the area at its tip, while a current of higher

destroy

intensity will ablate or _____ the area. This is called an *electrolytic lesion*.

hypothalamus
ablation,
   stimulation
ablation

8.11 The most important part of the limbic system for primary drives, the _____, may be studied by either _____ or _____. In _____ the tissue is actually destroyed, while in stimulation it is not.

ablated

8.12 If an area near the *center* of the hypothalamus is _____ or destroyed, there is a marked increase in appetite.

Animals eat voraciously and continuously, becoming extremely obese (Brobeck, 1946).

8.13 A lesion which _____ or ablates an area a fraction of an inch to one side of the center of the hypothalamus (i.e., in the lateral area) reduces appetite so completely that the animal will die of starvation while surrounded by food (Teitelbaum and Stellar, 1954).

destroys

8.14 Since a lesion near the center of the hypothalamus causes hunger to _____, it is thought that this area (when operating normally) functions to reduce or *inhibit* hunger. It is thus called an *inhibitory* center.

increase

8.15 Conversely, the lateral area, the ablation of which causes _____ hunger, is thought to be important in increasing or exciting the hunger drive. It is called an *excitatory* center for the hunger drive.

reduced

8.16 In light of the above evidence, it would appear that there are two hypothalamic areas concerned with the hunger drive. The central area is an _____ area, the lateral an _____ area.

inhibitory
excitatory

8.17 Further evidence comes from the *stimulation* technique. Stimulation of the *central* area, which is thought to _____ appetite, does, in fact, reduce hunger (Smith, 1961). Stimulation of the lateral area, on the other hand, increases the animal's appetite (Delgado and Anand, 1953; Miller, 1958).

inhibit (reduce)

8.18 The central area of the hypothalamus is thought to be an _____ center, since ablation of this area causes _____ hunger, while stimulation causes _____ hunger.

inhibitory

increased
decreased

8.19 The lateral area is called an _____ area for the hunger drive, since ablation of the area causes _____ hunger, while stimulation causes _____ hunger.

excitatory

reduced
increased

8.20 It has been pointed out that the hypothalamic centers concerned with hunger are *paired*. One is an _____ area, the principal concern of which is to _____ hunger. The other is an _____ center, which functions primarily to _____ hunger.

excitatory

increase
inhibitory
reduce

8.21 It should be noted that metabolism and other bodily functions are *normal* in animals with central or lateral hypothalamic lesions. The principal effect of these lesions is thus apparently on *appetite*, not on the homeostatic mechanisms of the body.

THIRST AND SEX

Hypothalamic influences on the thirst and sex drives have also been studied. A "thirst" center has been located in the hypothalamus. It is thought that this center is influenced by changes in osmotic pressure and that the center in turn influences the pituitary gland to maintain water balance. Evidence on the sex drive indicates that sexual responses are organized in the anterior hypothalamus.

8.22 The two methods used in studying the effect of the hypothalamus on hunger, _____ and _____, have also been used with *thirst*.

ablation,
    stimulation

8.22a Match each procedure on the left with its effect on the right by placing the correct number(s) in the blank beside each statement on the right. More than one number may be placed in each blank.

(1) Ablation of central hypothalamus

(2) Stimulation of lateral hypothalamus _____ increased appetite   1, 2

(3) Stimulation of central hypothalamus _____ decreased appetite   3, 4

(4) Ablation of lateral hypothalamus _____ no effect on appetite

8.23 Repeated electrical stimulation of a particular area of the hypothalamus in one experiment induced goats to *drink* excessive amounts of water (Andersson and McCann, 1955).

8.24 In a second experiment, destruction of this same area of the hypothalamus of dogs caused *reduced* water intake and eventually marked dehydration. (Andersson and McCann, 1956). As with hunger, this center would be called an (excitatory, inhibitory) center for thirst.   excitatory

8.25 A third method of investigating thirst functions involves the *injection* of minute quantities of *liquid* into the hypothalamus. Injection of a salt solution into particular areas causes an *increase* in drinking. Similar results have been found with goats (Andersson and McCann, 1955) and cats (Miller, 1957).

8.26 The experiments reported above indicate that injection of salt solution may _____ drinking. Conversely, other experiments have shown that injection of water into the same area may *decrease* drinking (Miller, 1957).

increase

8.27 The most prevalent theory of hypothalamic functioning proposes that there is a center in the hypothalamus which is sensitive to changes in osmotic pressure. An increase in *osmotic pressure* (such as that caused by salt injection) will cause _____ drinking; a decrease in pressure causes _____ drinking.

increased
decreased

8.28 Either electrical stimulation or injection of salt solution into a particular area causes _____ _____. On the other hand, ablation of this area or injection of water will _____ _____.

increased
drinking

reduce
drinking

8.29 Hypothalamic control of drinking is thought to be initiated by changes in _____ pressure. The influence of the hypothalamus on the *pituitary* gland is thought to be of prime importance in the control of water intake. The exact nature and extent of this influence is, however, not yet clearly established.

osmotic

8.30 Three methods have been used in studying the effect of the hypothalamus on water intake. These are _____, _____, and _____.

ablation
stimulation,
injection

8.31 It is thought that a hypothalamic "thirst" center is influenced by changes in _____ pressure and that this center may in turn directly influence the _____ gland, which is also of importance in the maintenance of body water balance.

osmotic

pituitary

8.32 The nature of hypothalamic influence on the *sex* drive has not been clearly established. However, evidence indicates that sexual responses are *organized* in the hypothalamus.

8.33 Restricted *lesions* in specific areas of the hypothalamus have been shown to *abolish* sexual behavior in both male and female animals, just as the ablation of the l_____ area of the hypothalamus reduces appetite.

lateral

8.34 *Injection* of *male hormone* into an anterior (front) part of the hypothalamus *induced* sexual behavior, though electrical stimulation of this area had no effect (Fisher, 1956). When the _____ method was employed, however, sexual behavior was eliminated.

ablation

8.35 It has been shown that sexual behavior is induced by the injection of _____ _____ into an _____ part of the hypothalamus.

male hormones
anterior

8.36 If the anterior hypothalamus is stimulated electrically, there is (increase, decrease, no change) in sexual behavior.

no change

8.37 Stimulation of the anterior hypothalamus by injected male hormones produces an

increase

decrease

_____ in sexual behavior, while ablation produces a _____.

8.38 Most evidence indicates that sexual responses are organized in the hypothalamus. This function is probably carried out

anterior

primarily in the _____ part of the hypothalamus.

8.38a State the three methods (in any order) commonly used to study hypothalamic functioning.

(1) stimulation

(2) ablation

(3) injection

(1) _____

(2) _____

(3) _____

THE LIMBIC SYSTEM AND REINFORCEMENT

In addition to its specific influences on primary drives, the limbic system serves as a center for positive and negative reinforcement. Experiments have demonstrated that animals will learn to perform particular responses in order to obtain electrical stimulation of certain parts of the hypothalamus and septum. Since the electrical stimulation thus increases the probability of a response, it is properly referred to as a positive reinforcer. In other areas, stimulation leads to increased avoidance responses and is hence a negative reinforcer.

8.39 The hypothalamus also functions importantly as a sleeping-waking mechanism, in the maintenance of optimal blood pressure and temperature, and in what is usually referred to as _emotional_ and _motivated_ behavior.

8.40 In connection with the latter, some important findings of recent years should be noted. In our earlier discussion of reinforcement, it was noted that any event which increases the probability of a particular response in a given situation is called a reinforcer. It was noted that reinforcers include food, water, and electric shock. It has been found that *stimulation* of specific loci in the *limbic system* can also act as reinforcement.

8.41 Centers throughout the limbic system, which include the _____, s_____, and a_____, can, when electrically stimulated, act as positive and negative reinforcement areas.

hypothalamus
septum,
   amygdala

8.42 In investigating positive and negative reinforcement centers, electrodes are implanted in the manner previously described (frame 8.10). An electrical cord can then be attached to the implanted electrode. The cord is attached to a bar in such a way that, when the animal presses the bar, a weak current is passed through the electrodes. This had been a principal method used in investigating the location of _____ and _____ reinforcement areas.

positive
negative

8.43 In experiments utilizing the implantation technique, Olds (1955, 1956, 1958) found that with certain electrode placements, particularly in the *septal* area and certain parts of the *hypothalamus*, rats would quickly learn to press the bar at extremely high rates (e.g., 2,000 times in twenty-six hours) in order to receive stimulation.

8.44 In Olds's experiments the rats would often

reinforcer

continue to press the bar to exhaustion. The fact that the rats would strive so hard for stimulation indicates that it acts as a _____ .

8.45 Other areas have been found in which the rat will learn to *avoid* stimulation.

negative

These would be _____ reinforcement areas, while those in which the animal strives for stimulation would be

positive

_____ reinforcement areas.

8.46 The hypothalamus, amygdala, and septum,

limbic system

which form the _____ _____ , are important centers for motivated and emotional behavior. The latter, which includes rage, fear, etc., will not be discussed here.

8.47 The hypothalamus has been shown to be

hunger
thirst, sex

important in the _____ , _____ , and _____ drives, as well as in sleep, blood pressure, and temperature.

positive
negative
   reinforcement
limbic

8.48 Olds's experiments have demonstrated the existence of _____ and _____ centers in the _____ system. This system may thus be said to be primarily concerned with the *organization* and to some degree *control* of motivated and emotional behavior.

8.49 The brain area which is thought to largely

limbic system
hypothalamus
amygdala,
   septum

control motivated behavior is the _____ _____ . It consists primarily of the _____ , _____ , and _____ .

8.50 The hypothalamus organizes and largely
controls behavior in response to the
_____ drives, such as hunger,
_____, and _____.
Its function in the maintenance of body
homeostasis also includes control over
sleep, b_____ p_____,
and t_____.

primary
  (physiological)
thirst, sex

blood pressure
temperature

8.51 The entire limbic system is involved in
_____ and _____
behavior. The most important part of this
system for the maintenance of homeostasis
appears to be the _____.

motivated,
  emotional

hypothalamus

8.51a State the primary drives and homeostatic
functions in which the hypothalamus is
important.
Drives: _____
Functions: _____
_____

Drives: hunger,
  sex, thirst
Functions: sleep,
  blood pressure,
  temperature

8.52 Olds found positive reinforcement centers
at various points in the _____
and _____.

hypothalamus
septum

8.52a What two types of centers did Olds find
in the limbic system?
_____

positive and
  negative rein-
  forcement

Activation and the RAS

For various reasons, including variation in presence and strength of operative drives at a given time, the organism does not remain constantly at the same level of activity or *activation*. Rather, the activation level varies from a very low point, such as sleep, to the high points found in states of extreme anger, fear, or excitement. These states of high activation may be referred to simply as states of *vigorous activity*. Most behavior, of course, falls in the middle ranges of the activation scale.

Although motivation and activation are not necessarily identical, they are *positively correlated*. That is, an organism that is highly motivated (i.e., whose behavior is energized by a drive) tends to have a high level of activation. Conversely, an organism with little motivation tends to be quiescent and is thus said to have a low level of activation.

9.1　At the lower extreme of the scale of activation is sleep. In a deep sleep the organism is maximally inactive and is said to be at
activation　　　　　its lowest level of _____.

9.2 While the lowest level of *activation* is _____, the upper extreme may be incurred in states of extreme anger, fear, or excitement. We have labeled this upper extreme of activation simply vigorous _____.

sleep

activity

9.3 Most normal behavior patterns are near the middle of the *activation* scale. The upper extreme, which we have called _____ _____, and the lower extreme, _____, occur with relative rarity.

vigorous activity
sleep

9.4 The individual who suddenly finds himself being chased by a wounded bear is likely to be at a very high level of _____. This same individual may, however, fall asleep later the same day (provided he effects an escape!). He will then be at a relatively low _____ of _____.

activation

level
activation

9.5 It was noted earlier that drives *energize* behavior. Research has indicated that this energizing function is very similar to what we have called activation. That is, highly motivated organisms tend to have high _____ of _____.

levels,
activation

9.6 Another way of stating this relationship is to say that there is a *positive correlation* between motivation and activation. In one experiment it was found that increasing the amount of money reinforcement for men performing a simple laboratory task increased their muscular tension (Bartoshuk, 1955). In this case, level of _____ was measured in terms of muscular tension, and money supplied the motivation.

activation

9.7 The example cited above indicates that an increase in motivation produces a corresponding increase in _____.
There is thus a positive _____ between _____ and activation.

activation
correlation
motivation

9.8 When the level of activation of an organism is low, its drive level or motivation would be expected to be _____.

low

9.9 It has been found that during relative relaxation there is a decrease in the leukocyte (white blood-cell) count, while during an examination the count increases. In this experiment the leukocyte count was a measure of _____ level.

activation

9.10 The above experiment gives further support to the finding that there is a _____ _____ between activation level and motivation.

positive
correlation

THE RETICULAR ACTIVATING SYSTEM

Numerous investigators have attempted to discover how the brain functions to influence, or even control, motivation and activation. One important neural (i.e., brain) area, the limbic system, was discussed in Chapter 8. As was noted, this neural system, and particularly the hypothalamus, exerts extensive influence over a number of specific primary drives. While the generalization may be too broad, we might say that the limbic system influences the *directive* components of primary drives.

The *energizing* aspect of drive may originate in another neural system, the *reticular activating system* (RAS). The RAS is a diffuse system of nerve fibers arising in the brainstem and extending upward to the hypothalamus and the cortex. Because it is diffuse and projects over a wide area of the cortex, the RAS is called a *nonspecific* system.

Using the electroencephalogram (EEG) to study electrical brain waves, investigators have compiled considerable evidence which indicates that the RAS is the neural basis of activation. For example, stimulation of the RAS produces EEG changes indicating a state of alertness. Conversely, surgical severing of the RAS fibers produces a state of extended somnolence.

9.11 The concept of activation level and its correlation with _____ have been applied to the functioning of the brain.

motivation

9.12 The activation level of the brain is studied by placing *electrodes* on the skull and recording *electrical waves* produced by the uppermost layer of the brain, the *cortex*. The record obtained is called an (electrocardiogram, electroneurogram, electroencephalogram).

electroencephalogram

9.13 It has been found that the electroencephalogram (EEG) pattern varies as a function of the activation level of the individual. When he is asleep, the pattern is slow. With increased activation or arousal, it becomes more rapid. The EEG, then, measures the _____ _____ of the individual.

activation level

9.14 Further studies, in which brain waves have been recorded with the _____, have shown that the reticular activating system (RAS) is responsible for the activation or arousal of the brain.

EEG

9.15 The RAS is a diffuse system of nerve fibers arising in the *brainstem*, running upward to the *hypothalamus*, and projecting to the

activate
(arouse)

brainstem
hypothalamus
cortex

nonspecific

activate

activates

cortex. Its principal function is to
_____ the brain.

9.16 Specific nerve tracts from the various
senses (vision, audition, etc.) terminate in
specific areas of the cortex. The RAS, however, receives collateral fibers from these
main nerve tracts and projects *diffusely* to
the entire cortex. It is therefore called a
nonspecific system.

9.17 The RAS arises in the _____,
runs to the _____, and projects
diffusely to the cerebral _____.
Because of its diffuse pathways, it is called
a _____ system.

9.18 The function of the nonspecific projection
system is to _____ the brain.

9.19 Moruzzi and Magoun (1949) implanted
electrodes in the RAS of cats and attached
other electrodes to the skull to record the
EEG. When the RAS was electrically
stimulated, they found that: (1) A sleep-
ing or drowsy cat awoke, and one already
awake became more alert; and (2) the
EEG was altered, the changes being the
same as those which take place upon wak-
ing or arousal.

9.20 Other evidence corroborating the hypothesis that the RAS _____ the brain
has been found by cutting the RAS sur-
gically. When this operation was performed
on cats, they became somnolent (drowsy)
for long periods of time, sometimes permanently (Lindsley, Bowden, and Magoun,
1950).

9.21 If the RAS is stimulated, cats become
_____; if it is severed, they be-
come _____. We might thus
conclude that the RAS is important in the
_____ of the organism.

aroused
(alerted,
    activated)
somnolent
    (drowsy)
activation

9.22 Stimulation of the RAS produces
EEG patterns which are indicative of
_____. The EEG is a recording
of the el_____ waves produced
by the _____ of the brain.

activation
    (arousal)
electrical
cortex

9.23 The RAS is a nonspecific system, arising
in the _____. Its fibers extend
to the _____ and project to the
_____ to activate the latter.

brainstem
hypothalamus
cortex

9.24 The RAS ties in closely with the
hypothalamus, amygdala, and septum,
which make up the _____
_____. Both are important in
m_____.

limbic
    system
motivation

9.25 Since the activation level has been shown
to be positively _____ with
motivation, and since activation is a function of the RAS, we may infer that *motivation* is likewise a function of the RAS.

correlated

9.26 Both the _____ and the
_____ system function in motivation of the organism. The former is important in the more general activation or
energizing aspect of motivation, while the
latter appears to be more concerned with
specific drives.

RAS
limbic

hunger
thirst, sex

RAS
activation

9.27 The limbic system is apparently important in the organization and control of specific drives, such as _____, _____, and _____, while the other motivational system, the _____, has as its principal function the _____ of the cortex.

9.28 Classify each of the following by indicating in the blank whether it is most closely related to the RAS, the limbic system, neither, or both.

(1) limbic
(2) RAS
(3) limbic
(4) limbic or
     both
(5) both
(6) RAS

(1) Directive component
    of drive   _____

(2) Energizing component
                                _____

(3) Septum   _____
(4) Hypothalamus   _____
(5) Motivation   _____
(6) Nonspecific   _____

9.29 The apparent analogy between the two neural (i.e., brain) systems which have been discussed and the two generally hypothesized functions of drives (energizing and directing) should not be carried too far for several reasons: (1) The neural mechanisms are much more complex than has been indicated here. The relationships may thus not be as straightforward as they appear to be. (2) The functioning of these neural mechanisms is not clearly understood as yet. (3) The systems mentioned can be fully understood only as they are interrelated with other parts of the brain and of the body as a whole. (4) The energizing and directing functions of drive are *hypothetical*. In fact, as we shall see in a later section, some theories, having a different point of view, treat drives in a way different from that in which we have thus far been treating them.

9.30 Particular senses, such as vision, send nerve tracts to definite loci in the brain. The RAS, however, is a _____ system, the principal concern of which is the _____ of the cortex.

nonspecific

activation

SECONDARY MOTIVATION: 10

Acquisition of Relatively Simple Motives

In contrast to primary drives, secondary motives are nonphysiological and learned. Although there is some disagreement about the processes through which motives are learned, two general types of learning may be distinguished. In both types, the organism learns a connection or relationship between a stimulus and a response. In the first learning process, called *classical conditioning,* the organism learns a connection between a new or conditioned stimulus (CS) and a new or conditioned response (CR). This learning is based on an unlearned connection between an unconditioned stimulus (UCS) and an unconditioned response (UCR). For learning of the CS-CR relationship to take place, the CS is consistently presented with the UCS. The UCS leads to a UCR. Through repeated presentations, the CS comes to elicit a response similar to the UCR. This new response is the CR. When conditioning (i.e., learning) has taken place, the CS will elicit a response (the CR) without the presentation of the UCS.

The second learning process, called *instrumental conditioning,* involves the reinforcement of emitted responses. In this type of learning the naïve organism initially makes a number of different responses in a given situation. In the simplest situation, one of these responses is rewarded (i.e., reinforced). The rewarded response will increase in probability and is thus said to be learned. The nonrewarded responses will drop out. The situation may, of course, be much more complex. For example, several responses, rather than just one, may be reinforced, or a particular response may be reinforced only under very specific conditions.

It is important to note that the basic difference between classical and instrumental conditioning is that the former involves the *elicitation* of responses which are then reinforced (by the UCS). Instrumental conditioning, on the other hand, involves no elicitation of response, but merely the reinforcement of one or more of the several responses emitted by the organism. This difference will become clearer in the frames which follow.

10.1 It has previously been noted that most motives can be conveniently divided into primary motives and _____ motives. Our discussion thus far has been principally concerned with primary motives. We shall now consider in some detail the development and operation of secondary motives.

    secondary

10.2 As was noted earlier, the two primary characteristics of secondary _____ are that they are usually *nonphysiological* and that they are *learned*.

    motives

10.3 Secondary motives are distinguished from primary motives in that the former are based on the experience of the organism. It would thus be expected that secondary motives are both _____ and _____.

    nonphysiological, learned

THE LEARNING PROCESS

10.4 Although a detailed discussion of the psychology of learning is beyond the scope of this text, it is necessary to preface our discussion of the learning of secondary motives with a brief consideration of some of the principal processes which operate to allow the organism to learn motives on the basis

experience

of its _____.

Classical conditioning

experience
(learning)

10.5 Many secondary drives, based on the _____ of the organism, are acquired through a process called *classical conditioning*. The classical conditioning situation has four important components: the *unconditioned stimulus* (UCS), the *unconditioned response* (UCR), the *conditioned stimulus* (CS), and the *conditioned response* (CR).

10.6 The UCS is an *unlearned* stimulus to which the organism makes an *unlearned* response (the UCR). For example, if food (UCS) is presented to a hungry dog, it will salivate (UCR). Both UCS and UCR are components of the

classical
conditioning

_____ _____ situation.

10.7 The CS is a previously neutral stimulus which has been consistently paired with (presented just before) the UCS and has come to elicit a response very similar to the UCR. This response is the CR. Of these, the UCR is an unlearned response, while the CR is _____.

learned

10.8 In the example given above, if the experimenter rings a bell just before presenting the food and this bell comes to elicit a salivary response similar to the UCR, the bell is called the _____ and the organism's response is the _____.

CS
CR

10.9 Consider the following experiment: The experimenter places a rat in a box and gives him repeated shocks which cause the rat to jump. In the first stage of the experiment, each shock is preceded by the presentation of a brief light. In the second stage, the light alone elicits a jumping response from the rat. In the experiment described, the light is a _____, the shock a _____.

CS
UCS

10.10 In the experiment above, the rat's jumping response to the shock is a _____, while the jumping response to the light is the _____.

UCR
CR

10.11 The two stimulus elements of the classical conditioning situation are the _____ and the _____, while the two response elements are the _____ and the _____.

CS, UCS

CR, UCR

10.11a In the blank following each component of the classical paradigm, indicate whether it is learned or unlearned:
(1) CR _____
(2) UCS _____
(3) UCR _____
(4) CS _____

(1) learned
(2) unlearned
(3) unlearned
(4) learned

Instrumental conditioning

10.12 A second learning process involved in the learning of some _____

secondary

motives is *instrumental conditioning*. In this paradigm, the organism initially makes a number of different responses to a situation. Those which consistently bring reinforcement will be learned. Those which do not will drop out.

10.13 The experiment described in our discussion of reinforcement, in which the rat learned to press a lever for food, is an example of the learning process known
instrumental   as _____ conditioning.

10.14 The basic difference between classical and instrumental conditioning is that in the former responses are *elicited* from the subject by presenting a CS or UCS, while in instrumental conditioning the subject is allowed to emit responses
reinforced   which, if correct, are _____.

10.15 A common example of instrumental conditioning is seen in the crying of the baby. The infant's initial cries are simply a part of his response repertoire, which may also include kicking, smiling, laughing, etc. If the mother feeds the baby only when it cries, the infant will soon learn to cry when hungry. The crying is
emitted   thus an e_____ response which is reinforced.

10.16 The *elicitation* of particular responses by stimuli to which they are conditioned is basic to the paradigm of
classical   _____ conditioning.

10.17 The reinforcement of specific, *emitted*

responses is basic to the paradigm of
_____ conditioning.

instrumental

10.18   Both classical and instrumental conditioning can be important in the learning of _____ motives.

secondary

10.18a State the basic difference between classical and instrumental learning.
Classical: _____

_____

_____

Instrumental: _____

_____

Refer to
frame 10.14.

_____

Stimulus generalization

10.19   *Stimulus generalization*, or simply *generalization*, may be defined as the
tendency to respond in the same manner to all similar stimulus situations. Most
learned responses exhibit a tendency to
generalize.

10.20   Generalization occurs in both classical
conditioning, where responses are
elicited by the _____ or UCS,

CS

and instrumental conditioning, where
responses are _____.

emitted

10.21   In a classical conditioning situation
where the CS is a light of a certain
wavelength (hue), the organism will tend
to make the same response to similar
hues. This is an example of stimulus
_____.

generalization

10.22   The greater the dissimilarity between
the original CS and the generalization

stimulus, the *weaker* will be the tendency to respond to the latter. Thus,
the more similar the two stimuli, the
_____ the generalization.

greater
(stronger)

10.23 If a child is bitten by a large black dog,
he may subsequently exhibit fear of
other dogs. His fear of the dog which
originally bit him is simply due to the
establishment of a conditioned response.
The fear of other dogs is due to
_____.

generalization

10.24 If we observe the child, we find that he
fears a large brown dog more than he
fears a small white dog. This is probably
because the large brown dog is more
_____ to the large black dog
which originally bit him.

similar

10.25 The weaker fear response to the small
dog is probably due to the fact that
there is _____ stimulus generalization to stimuli less similar to the
original stimulus.

less (weaker)

SIMPLE SECONDARY MOTIVES

Approach motives

The approach-avoidance classification of drives discussed in Chapter
1 can be readily applied to secondary motives. A secondary approach
motive is simply a learned drive which motivates the organism to
approach a secondary positive goal. A secondary avoidance motive
leads the organism to avoid a secondary avoidance goal. Both approach
and avoidance motives may be learned through either classical or
instrumental conditioning.

10.26 Secondary drives, like primary, may be
divided into appetitive and aversive

motives. The terms appetitive and aversive are synonymous with approach and
_____.

avoidance

10.27 It will be recalled that food, which is the object of the rat's hunger-motivated behavior, is a g_____. In the same way, a secondary approach motive has a *secondary positive goal*.

goal

10.28 A famous experiment in secondary approach motivation was performed by Wolfe (1936) and later verified by Cowles (1937). In the first stage of his experiment, Wolfe taught chimpanzees to insert white poker chips into a machine to obtain grapes. In Stage II, Wolfe forced the chimps to pull a heavy weight to obtain chips. The fact that the chimps worked for poker chips indicates that the chips had become a secondary
_____.

goal

10.29 The Wolfe experiment demonstrated the development of a secondary _____ motive. The grapes were primary _____, while the poker chips were _____ _____.

approach
(positive)
goals
secondary
goals

10.30 Most people are willing to work quite hard in order to earn money which will purchase food, clothing, etc., and, in general, indirectly satisfy their needs. Money, which is physically merely pieces of paper and metal, is a _____ goal for these people.

secondary

10.31 Secondary goals, such as poker chips

learning or money, are acquired through _____, while primary goals are based on the physiological needs of the organism.

10.32 Suppose that Wolfe's chimps had been taught to insert white chips into the vending machine and that later only yellow chips were available. If it were found that the chimps were willing to work for yellow chips, we would have an example of the process of

generalization _____.

10.33 If an organism learns to make instrumental responses in order to obtain a secondary

secondary goal, we say that he has developed a
approach _____ _____ motive.

Avoidance motives

10.34 The poker chips in the study cited above were an example of a secondary positive

learned goal of a _____ approach motive. A more extensively investigated phenomenon than the secondary approach motive has been the *secondary avoidance motive*, generally in the form of a *learned fear* drive.

secondary 10.35 Since fear is an aversive drive and is
avoidance learned, it is called a _____
(aversive) _____ motive.

10.36 One of the most important studies
learned demonstrating that fear is a l_____ drive was performed by Miller (1948). Miller's apparatus consisted of a box with two compartments, one painted black, the other white. A door with horizontal

black and white stripes separated the two compartments. In addition, the floor of the white compartment was a metal grid through which shock could be delivered to the rats which were used as subjects.

10.37 Because of the importance of this study, the several stages of the experiment will be described in some detail and the implications of each noted. Fear was first operationally defined as excessive defecation and urination, tenseness, and crouching. In Stage I, the rats were *tested* to assure that they did not exhibit any fear of the apparatus in terms of these indices of fear. This was done to assure that fear was a _____ drive, not a primary drive.

secondary (learned)

10.38 In Stage II, the rats were given a number of electric shocks through the grid in the white box. Following this *fear conditioning*, the subjects exhibited fear (in terms of the indices noted above) in the white box, even when no shocks were being given. This is an indication that they had _____ to fear the white compartment.

learned

10.39 The learning involved in Stage II is an example of (classical, instrumental) conditioning.

classical

10.40 Recall that the important elements of the classical conditioning paradigm are the UCS, CS, UCR, and CR. In the fear conditioning stage described above, the fearful behavior of the rats in the white box was both the _____ and

UCR

CR
CS
UCS

primary

learned

drive

instrumental

learned
  (secondary)

No shocks were

the _____. The white box was the _____. The shock was the _____.

10.41 Having demonstrated that fear is not a _____ drive but rather a learned drive, Miller wanted to discover whether or not fear has the properties of a primary drive. Specifically, he wanted to know whether or not fear can mediate the learning of a *new response*. In Stage III, the apparatus was set up so that the rat could open the door and escape from the white compartment into the black by turning a wheel above the door. The rats were placed in the white box and made a number of responses until, by chance, they turned the wheel and escaped into the black box. The subjects soon learned to turn the wheel as soon as they were placed in the white compartment, indicating that learned fear is a *drive*. It is important to note that during this *new learning* stage of the experiment, *no* additional shocks were given.

10.42 In the fear conditioning stage (II), Miller found that fear is _____. In the new response stage (III), he showed that fear is a _____, in that it mediates new learning.

10.43 The learning involved in Stage III is an example of (classical, instrumental) conditioning in which the learning of a new response was mediated by a _____ avoidance drive.

10.44 How can we be certain that the escape

response learned in Stage III was based on a secondary drive (i.e., fear) and not on a primary drive (i.e., pain)?

given during Stage III, and there was thus no pain involved.

_____

_____

10.45 The two most important implications of the Miller experiment are that fear is _____ and that it acts as a _____. The properties of fear can thus be summarized by saying that it is a _____ avoidance _____.

learned
drive
secondary
(learned)
motive
(drive)

10.46 A second important experiment was performed by Watson and Raynor (1920). These investigators presented a child with a loud, noxious sound in the presence of a white rat. The child subsequently exhibited fear of the rat, although it had previously shown no fear. This experiment again demonstrated that fear is _____.

learned

10.47 An important additional finding of the Watson and Raynor study was that after the white rat was paired with noxious stimulation, the child feared not only the rat but also other furry animals. This was probably due to the process of stimulus g_____.

generalization

10.48 The important points of the Watson and Raynor experiment are that it demonstrated: (1) that fear can be conditioned in human beings and (2) that the fear response _____ to similar stimuli.

generalizes

10.49 What type of conditioning was used in the Watson and Raynor experiment?

classical

_____

10.50 It has been pointed out that both a_____ and _____ motives can be learned. When either type is learned, it is called a

approach,
  avoidance
secondary drive
  (learned motive)

_____ _____.

10.51 There is one important difference between secondary approach motives and secondary avoidance motives. When a secondary approach motive has been established on the basis of a primary drive, as was the case in the chimp experiment, it is necessary to give primary reinforcement periodically, or the secondary drive will no longer operate. In the Wolfe (1936) study cited above this would mean that if food reinforcement were not given periodically, the chimps would stop working for poker chips. This process is called *extinction*. In the case of a learned *avoidance* (fear) drive, however, the drive, once established, is often very difficult to extinguish. Even without primary reinforcement (e.g., shock), the learned fear drive will continue to operate.

10.52 Several important experiments dealing with the extinction of avoidance drives will be discussed. In the first, Miller (1951) employed an apparatus similar to the one described above. The fear conditioning procedure employed in the earlier study was carried out, and the rats were subsequently tested without additional shocks. Results showed that some rats continued to make instrumental escape responses for more than 600 trials without primary reinforcement (i.e., shock).

10.53 The Miller (1951) experiment demonstrated that a conditioned fear-motivated response is often difficult to _____. The extinction of a secondary _____ response, on the other hand, is relatively easy.

extinguish
approach

10.54 The conditioned fear drive has been established in species other than the rat. Solomon and Wynne (1953) placed dogs in a two-compartment apparatus and administered shocks of traumatic intensity. The dog could avoid the shock by quickly leaping over a hurdle into the adjoining compartment. After ten successive avoidances, the shock was discontinued. The dogs, however, continued to perform the hurdle-jumping response for hundreds of trials without shock. Like the Miller experiment, this study demonstrated the difficulty of _____ a conditioned fear drive.

extinguishing

10.55 A third study has been carried out by Campbell, Sanderson, and Laverty (1964). These investigators used human subjects. Their procedure was to sound a tone followed by the administration of a drug, scoline, which causes a momentary blockage of respiration. The experience was considered by all subjects to be quite traumatic, and a conditioned response, including struggling, was established to the tone in a single trial. Although numerous extinction trials, presenting the tone alone, were carried out, the CR *never* extinguished.

10.56 Three important aspects of the Campbell et al. study are that: (1) _____ subjects were used; (2) a CR was established in _____ trial(s); and (3) the CR _____ extinguished.

Human

one
never

10.57 Taken together, the Miller (1951), Solomon and Wynne (1953), and Campbell et al. (1964) studies indicate that conditioned _____ is a strong drive which is difficult to _____.

fear
extinguish

10.58 Four types of drive have been discussed. The hunger drive is a _____ _____ motive; the pain drive is a _____ _____ drive; the striving of the chimps to obtain poker chips represents the operation of a _____ _____ drive; and the fear drive is a _____ _____ drive.

primary
   approach
primary avoidance

secondary
   approach
secondary
   avoidance

10.59 A major difference between approach and avoidance motives is that the latter are generally much more resistant to _____.

extinction

Achievement Motivation 11

In Chapter 10 we briefly considered the operation of several specific secondary motives. In the present chapter, we shall discuss in somewhat greater detail the operation and measurement of an important type of motivation in our society, *achievement motivation*. Middle-class American society has often been described as an achieving society. The social group as a whole places high value both on striving to achieve and on achievement itself. It is thus true that achievement motivation is socially, as well as financially, *rewarded* in our culture.

The individual in an achieving society may react to social pressure to achieve in any of at least three ways. He may: remain static, strive to achieve success, or strive to avoid failure. Of the latter two alternatives, the first is an approach motive, the second an avoidance motive.

Fairly extensive theory and research have been developed around the approach-avoidance distinction. In the frames which follow, we shall consider some aspects of the theory, as well as several of the experiments which have attempted to test the theory.

11.1 Although the society in general places

achievement

high value on _____ motivation, this motive may be of particular importance to the college student. It is known that the degree of motivation to achieve can make the critical difference between success and failure in college.

11.2 Two students, X and Y, are of equal ability and have had similar previous education. If both are taking a particularly difficult course and X has higher

motivation

achievement _____, it is likely that he will do better in the course than will Y.

rewards

11.3 The society socially _____ strong achievement motivation. It is thus a highly valued motive in our society. For this reason, it is important to consider it in some detail.

11.4 The individual who is a member of middle-class American society is constantly in what we call an *achievement situation*. This is simply a situation in which achievement and striving for achievement are highly *valued* activities and are thus socially rewarded.

11.5 Since the individual is forced by his society membership into an

achievement

_____ situation, he is also forced to react behaviorally to the situation in one or more of three ways. He may (1) remain static, (2) strive to *achieve success*, or (3) strive to *avoid failure*.

11.6 If the individual remains static, he, in

effect, does not worry about the situation. He simply does not care what the society thinks of his achievements or lack of same. The static individual has relatively low _____ _____.

achievement motivation

11.7   The other two possible reactions represent the more usual sides of the achievement coin. The striving for success is what has previously been described as an *approach* motive, while the striving against failure represents an *avoidance* motive.

11.8   The negative striving against failure or _____ motive is called a *fear-of-failure* or simply a failure-avoidance motive.

avoidance

11.9   It has been hypothesized that some individuals characteristically exhibit an achievement motive, while others are usually motivated by negative failure- _____ motivation. The former are called the *hope-of-success* or *HS* individuals, while the latter are called *fear-of-failure* or *FF* individuals (McClelland, Atkinson, Clark, and Lowell, 1953).

avoidance

11.10   The striving toward success, or _____ motive, is characteristic of the _____ type of individual. This type of person has a *positive* attitude toward achievement situations.

achievement hope-of- success

11.11   Middle-class American society is an

achievement

_____ situation. The individual who is motivated to avoid failure in this situation is an FF (fear-of-failure) individual.

primary

11.12 Just as the pain drive is a _____ avoidance motive, fear-of-failure is a

secondary

_____ avoidance motive.

THE DEVELOPMENT OF ACHIEVEMENT MOTIVATION

11.13 According to the theory of McClelland et al. (1953), the achievement or

approach

_____ motive develops out of the *growing expectations* of the child.

11.14 When a child approaches a new achievement situation, such as a mechanical puzzle, he has no expectations concerning his ability to manipulate the puzzle. If the puzzle is not too difficult and he is able to manipulate it correctly, he soon develops certain expectations and derives pleasure from these expectations. Success in the achievement situation and in predicting the outcome of the situation provides *positive reinforcement* for the developing achievement motive. Eventually, the child develops 100 percent expectations of achievement in manipulating the puzzle. At this point, the puzzle loses its novelty, and its manipulation is no longer considered an achievement. The achievement-conscious parent should, at this time, provide a new and slightly more complex situation. If he does this, the child will have renewed interest in achievement, and his development of achievement motivation will progress. In McClelland's theory, then, in order to develop an achievement motive, the child must get *pleasure* (positive reinforcement). To get pleasure, he must be exposed to *increasingly more complex* objects and situations which nevertheless permit mastery.

11.15   The positive achievement motive is called *need achievement* or *nAch*. For this motive to develop adequately, objects to which the child is exposed must be increasingly more _____.   complex

If the child masters these objects and situations, he experiences _____.   pleasure

11.16   If situations are constantly too complex, the child may experience *negative affect* and develop not an achievement motive but a failure-avoidance motive.

11.17   If the child is able, with some effort, to master his puzzle, he will experience

_____ and tend to develop   pleasure

an _____ _____. If unable   achievement

to master it, he will experience   motive

_____ affect and will tend to   negative

develop a _____ motive.   failure-avoidance

11.18   What is needed for the development of nAch is the mastery of increasingly

_____ _____ situa-   more complex

tions. The individual whose development conforms to this pattern is likely to become a hope-of-_____   success

person.

11.19   If situations are consistently too complex for the child to master, he may become an _____ individual.   FF

11.20 The mastery of increasingly more complex situations leads to _____, which reinforces _____ achievement and helps the child to develop into an _____ individual.

pleasure
need

HS

11.21 The two types of achievement motivation are (nAch and fear-of-failure *or* approach and avoidance).

Either is
correct.

MEASUREMENT OF THE ACHIEVEMENT MOTIVE

11.22 It would seem worthwhile to develop some means of measuring a motive so important as the achievement motive. Such a measure has been developed by McClelland et al. (1953). The method of measurement employed by these investigators has been the modified *Thematic Apperception Test* or *TAT*. The test consists of a series of rather vague pictures. The pictures are presented to a group and each person is asked to write a story about each picture. The stories are subsequently analyzed by trained scorers according to a scoring system designed to measure strength of the achievement motivation. A total achievement score is obtained for each individual, and the achievement scores can then be compared with other measures (intelligence, aspirations, etc.) or be used to subdivide the group on the basis of strength of the achievement motivation.

11.23 The test employed by McClelland to measure achievement motive is a modified _____ _____ Test. Al-

Thematic
Apperception

though it would be impossible to give here a complete description of research to date with the TAT, we will cite several exemplary studies and results.

11.24   In an early study, Clark and McClelland (1950) gave subjects the TAT and an anagrams test. It was found that all subjects except those high on nAch sagged midway through the anagrams test.

11.25   The study cited above indicated that high need _____ relates to more continuous striving on an anagrams task.   achievement

11.26   A second study is that of Atkinson (1950). This investigator gave subjects the TAT and asked them to estimate their grades on the final exam in a course. It was found that subjects high in nAch expected higher scores on the exam when the discrepancy between course grade and overall average was greater. The finding was interpreted as an indication that the more *ambiguous* the situation, the greater is the influence of nAch on expectations.

11.27   It would appear that achievement motivation has greater influence on expectations in more _____ situations.   ambiguous

11.28   Studies cited thus far have shown that high nAch promotes _____   higher
expectations and more continuous
_____ to achieve in certain   striving
situations.

118

11.29 McClelland et al. (1953) have reported several studies in which the relationship between nAch and college grades was calculated. One study found a significant correlation of .51 between nAch and college grades. This means that in that study a fairly good relationship between the two existed. Another study, however, showed a correlation of only .05 between nAch and grades. This correlation indicates that there is almost no relationship at all between the two. The general conclusion must be that the college grade–nAch relationship is an indefinite and probably variable one and that, in any case, so many factors other than nAch affect grades that the relationship can probably never be extremely high.

indefinite

higher
ambiguous

11.30 The relationship of nAch to college grades is a(n) _____ one. High nAch, according to the Atkinson (1950) study, leads subjects to expect _____ grades in more _____ situations.

strive

11.31 Clark and McClelland (1950) found that subjects high on nAch _____ more continuously than other subjects on an anagrams task.

continuous
expectations
college
 grades

11.32 To summarize the above studies, we might conclude that high nAch promotes more _____ striving and higher _____ and has an indefinite relationship to _____ _____.

11.32a State two effects (in any order) of high nAch.

(1) _____

(2) _____

(1) more continuous striving

(2) higher expectations

MEASUREMENT OF THE FAILURE-AVOIDANCE MOTIVE

11.33 The negative or avoidance motive is called the failure-avoidance or _____ - of - _____ motive, and the individual whose characteristic behavior patterns indicate domination by the failure-avoidance motive is called an _____ individual.

fear, failure

FF

11.34 Several theories and attempts to measure the FF motive have been made (Atkinson, 1957; Atkinson and Litwin, 1960; Birney, Burdick, and Teevan, 1964; Moulton, 1958). We will be concerned here, however, only with the system developed by Birney et al. (1964).

11.35 The *hostile press* or *HP* system, as the Birney et al. system is called, was developed to measure the strength of FF motivation. It has been the subject of a number of studies in which the system has been validated and the characteristics of failure-avoiding individuals determined. ·Like the McClelland system for nAch, the HP system employs a modified TAT or _____ _____ _____. Although the scoring criteria are different, the basic method of measuring HP is exactly the same as that for the achievement motive.

Thematic Apperception Test

11.36 In one study (Birney, Burdick, and Teevan, 1960), it was found that subjects who had experienced *failure* on a speed-reading task before taking the TAT showed more HP than did subjects who had not experienced such failure. Since a higher HP score indicates more _____ - of - _____ motivation, the finding supported the HP scoring system.

fear, failure

11.37 In the above-mentioned study, the experience of _____ increased the HP score. In another study, Hancock and Teevan (1964) found that subjects high on HP were more *irrational* in their performance on a risk-taking task.

failure

11.38 Teevan and Hartsough (1964) found that high-HP subjects are more anxious about failure than are lows, whereas Hancock and Teevan found that high-HP subjects are more _____.

irrational

11.39 Finally, Smith and Teevan (1964) found that college students who are high on HP do not view themselves as being as close to their ideal selves as do low-HP subjects. Teevan and Hartsough found that high-HP subjects are more _____ about failure.

anxious

FF

11.40 Subjects high on HP are _____, as opposed to HS individuals. According to the Smith and Teevan study, the high-HP subjects view themselves as being not close to their _____.

ideals

failure

11.41 Birney et al. found that _____ preceding the TAT increased HP scores;

i.e., it induced more _____ of   fear
_____ in the subjects.   failure

11.42 To summarize the research cited above,
we might say that (1) failure preceding
the TAT increases _____   HP
score, (2) high-HP individuals are more
_____ on a risk-taking task,   irrational
and (3) high-HP subjects view themselves as being farther from their
_____ than do low-HP sub-   ideals
jects.

11.43 As with nAch, the summary of research
on the HP system is far from complete.
The discussion here is designed only to
give the reader a sample of the type of
experimental investigation of human
motivation which has been and can be
done.

11.44 State three experimental findings (in
any order) concerning HP.
(1) _____   (1) Failure preced-
_____   ing TAT
_____   increases HP
_____   score.
(2) _____   (2) High HP indi-
_____   viduals are
_____   more irra-
_____   tional on a
_____   risk-taking
_____   task.
(3) _____   (3) High HP sub-
_____   jects view
_____   themselves as
_____   being farther
_____   from their
_____   ideals than do
_____   low HP
                                                subjects.

Complex Secondary Motives   12

Psychologists have long been concerned with the question of whether or not some secondary motives can continue to function without periodic primary reinforcement. Allport (1937) suggests that they can. He holds that some motives become *functionally autonomous,* meaning that they become independent of primary reinforcement.

learned

12.1 Secondary drives have thus far been considered l_____ drives based on
physiological drives.

12.2 In the Wolfe study, the secondary drive
to obtain poker chips was based on the
hunger drive. In the shock experiments, the
secondary fear drive was based on

pain

primary

the _____ drive, which is a
_____ drive.

12.3 If the chimps in Wolfe's experiment did
not receive food for their chips period-

ically, the drive for chips would soon be
_____.   extinguished

12.4 By functional autonomy, Allport means
    that the functionally autonomous motives
    continue to function without being period-
    ically reinforced by the reduction of a
    physiological drive.

12.5 The pauper who first earns money to satiate
    his hunger may continue to work long hours
    even after he has made his fortune. Since
    his secondary motivation is no longer rein-
    forced directly by the satisfaction of a
    primary motive, the motivation may be said
    to be functionally _____.   autonomous

12.6 A functionally autonomous motive is
    one which has become independent of   physiological
    _____ drives.   (primary)

12.7 Sexual desire may continue to be present
    after menopause. This constitutes another   functionally
    example of a _____ _____   autonomous
    motive.

ACQUISITION OF SOCIAL MOTIVES

Many secondary motives are learned through experience and interaction with people. Motives learned through this process of interpersonal interaction are termed *social motives*.

According to predominant psychological theories, the initial development of social motives takes place in infancy. The infant's helplessness and consequent dependence on others for need satisfaction
necessitates interpersonal interaction. As the infant develops, four
primary relationships and hence four sources of social motivational
development can be distinguished. The earliest of these is most commonly the infant-mother relationship. The second interaction occurs
between the infant and the family as a whole, since, second to the

mother, the infant is maximally dependent upon the family for need satisfaction. The third source for motive development is the larger social community, in which the growing child must interact with both peers and elders in order to learn social skills. The final motive source is formal education, in which the child learns social motives through direct education by parents, teachers, and others.

12.8 Many motives which become functionally autonomous are social motives. A *social motive* is simply one which involves, in its development and manifestation, *interpersonal interaction*.

12.9 Since social motives are learned through interpersonal interaction, they are

secondary

_____ motives. Examples include affiliation, achievement, etc. Some of these will be discussed in greater detail later.

12.10 The basis for the initial development of social motives is the infant's helplessness and consequent *dependence* upon others for the satisfaction of needs. Need satis-

interpersonal

faction thus necessitates _____ interaction, particularly with the mother.

interpersonal
interaction

12.11 The infant-mother relationship is the initial _____ _____ upon which the acquisition of social motives is based. The second source of social motives is the family as a whole, including both parents, brothers, and sisters.

12.12 The infant's initial relationship with the family, as with the mother, is one of

dependence

_____ upon the family. The child is thus forced to interact with the members of his family in order to satisfy his needs.

12.13 The mechanism through which the family aids in the development of social motives is called _____ _____. It is the same mechanism which operated in the infant's initial relationship with the _____.

interpersonal
interaction

mother

12.14 The first two sources for the development of social motives are the _____ and the _____. A third source is the larger *social community*.

mother, family

12.15 In the young child, a particularly significant segment of the social community is *playmates*. The relationship of the child to the mother and family was one of d_____.

dependence

12.16 While the child's relationship to _____ and _____ was primarily one of dependence, his relationship to his peers is better described as *mutual interdependence*. This simply means that each child contributes something to the satisfaction of the other's needs.

mother, family

12.17 The child's relationship to his peers is particularly significant in the learning of *social skills*. The latter may be described for our purposes as techniques of social interaction.

12.18 The basic process in the development of social motives, as with other secondary

learning

interpersonal
interaction

mother, family
social community

dependence
social
  community
mutual
  interdependence

social skills

social

mutually
  interdependent

Former is
  dependence;
latter is
  mutual inter-
  dependence.

interpersonal
  interaction

motives, is I_____. As distinguished from other secondary motives,
social motives are those whose development involves _____

_____.

12.19 Three sources of the interaction necessary for social motive development are
the _____, the _____,
and the _____ _____.

12.20 The child's early relationship to mother
and family is one of _____,
while his relationship with his peers in the
larger _____ _____
is one of_____ _____.

12.21 Through peer interaction, the child develops more adequate techniques of
social interaction. These techniques are
called _____ _____.

12.22 The _____ skills which the
child learns through interaction with
his playmates are based on a
_____ _____ rela-
tionship between the child and his peers.

12.23 What is the basic difference between
the infant-mother relationship and the
child-peer relationship?

_____

_____

12.24 A final source of development of social
motives is the deliberate education of
the child. As with the other sources,
_____ _____ is
necessary for the development of social
motives through education.

12.25 The education of the child in developing social motives is carried out first by the *parents* and later by the child's *teachers*.

12.26 A relatively formal mode of acquisition of social motives is _____.   education
This particular mode involves the interaction of the child principally with
_____ and _____.   parents, teachers

12.27 In general, social motives are learned through _____ _____.   interpersonal interaction
The four principal sources for the development of these motives are:
_____, _____,   mother, family
_____ _____ and   social community
_____.   education

12.28 It is important to note that the development of any given social motive may involve *any or all* of the four sources discussed.

12.29 Of the four sources of social motive development, the one involving the greatest degree of mutual interdependence is the child's interaction with the
_____ _____. The   social community (playmates)
earliest source of development is interaction with the _____.   mother

12.29a State the four primary sources of social motive development.   (1) mother
(1) _____   (2) family
(2) _____   (3) social
(3) _____   community
(4) _____   (4) education

COMPLEX MOTIVES

The affiliation motive

12.30 Having discussed the development of social motives in general, we shall now consider two specific motives which are of particular importance in understanding human motivation.

12.31 One of the most important and universal of human motives is the tendency to seek the companionship of others. This motive is called *affiliation*. Like other social motives, it is learned through

interpersonal
interaction

_____   _____.

12.32 There are various types of affiliation, some of which have received specific names. Marriage is one of these. An obvious partial basis for marriage is the sex drive. As a social motive, however, the affiliation involved in marriage is

learned

l_____.

12.33 The affiliative relationship involved in marriage entails, for most people, much more than the satisfaction of the sex drive. Among other things, marriage helps to satisfy a *dependency* drive, a drive to have other individuals upon whom one can depend.

12.34 It is thus seen that the affiliation motive may have various bases. In the case of marriage, two prominent contributors

sex
dependency

are the _____ drive and the _____ drive.

12.35 The dependency drive is also important in affiliative relationships other than marriage. The parent-child relationship has already been discussed. The child's tendency to maintain a close relationship to his parents is, in large part, based on the _____ drive.

dependency

12.36 As has been noted, the affiliation motive is almost universal in human societies. The probable reason for this is that affiliation satisfies a large number of different drives. Examples of these drives include the _____ _____ and the _____ _____.

sex
   drive
dependency
   drive

12.37 Another drive often underlying affiliation is the *status motive*. This is simply the motive to attain rank or status in the social group.

12.38 The operation of a status motive often underlies the affiliation involved in joining clubs and organizations. Status is a s_____ motive which is _____.

social
learned

12.38a What are the two motives which often underlie the affiliation motive?
   (1) _____
   (2) _____

(1) dependency
(2) status

12.39 The affiliation motive is almost _____ among human cultures because it satisfies a number of drives, including _____, _____, and _____.

universal
sex
dependency,
   status

12.40 Why is affiliation so widespread among human societies?
_____

It satisfies a
   number of
   drives.

The status motive

affiliation

12.41 It has already been noted that the status drive is one basis for the _____ motive. Most individuals in our culture strive for some status in the social group.

social

12.42 Status may be thought of as the individual's perceived *position* or *rank* in the social group of which he is a member. The motive to attain high status is a _____ motive.

status

12.43 One of the most obvious cases in which striving to attain a higher rank or _____ is important is the armed services. Here rank is important not only within the scope of military operations but at social gatherings as well.

position

12.44 The status motive involves primarily a striving to attain high rank or p_____ in the social group.

12.45 An extension of the status drive is the striving for power or *power motive*. The motive needs little discussion. It may be seen in the excessively strict father and the industrialist who rules his firm with an "iron hand."

rank (position)
power

12.46 The status motive may operate merely as a drive to attain a higher _____ or as a drive to attain _____ over others. There are also other forms of this social motive.

12.47 The young businessman who strives hard to obtain the vice-presidency in order to impress his friends is exhibiting, in part at least, a _____ _____. He may also desire to occupy a position in which he has control over a greater number of individuals. In this case his striving is also an attempt to satisfy a _____ motive. It can readily be seen that the two motives are often closely related.

status
motive

power

12.48 Affiliation and status have been discussed as two examples of _____ _____ which are acquired through _____. Many other examples are possible. In a later section, we will discuss in some detail the operation of motives in achievement situations.

social
motives
learning

CULTURAL VARIATION OF MOTIVES

We do not wish to convey the impression that all social motives develop and operate in the same manner for all human beings. There is, in fact, considerable variation as a function of culture. The affiliation motive, for example, while essentially universal, varies in degree and manifestation from one culture to another. Status and power motives are almost nonexistent in some cultures and very strong in others.

12.49 The operation of most motives, particularly social motives, is a function of the cultural setting in which the motive is manifested. In general, social motives vary considerably from one culture to another. This variation is largely due to the fact that these are secondary motives which are _____.

learned

12.50 It has been noted that the affiliation motive is found in all cultures and is essentially universal. This does not mean, however, that it does not vary in *degree* or *manifestation* with the culture. The affiliation is learned from others through _____ _____.

interpersonal
interaction

12.51 In our culture, for example, mothers are expected to love and care for infants, that is, to exhibit an affiliation motive with the infant as the object of affiliation. In some primitive cultures where an equal number of girls and boys in a family is considered ideal, "extra" infants of either sex are killed.

12.52 The above example of *infanticide* in a primitive society indicates that some motives _____ with the culture.

vary

12.53 Other motives vary to an even greater degree. Among the *Zuni* of New Mexico, the status and power motives are seemingly almost nonexistent (Benedict, 1934). This lack of status motivation and the _____ committed by the primitive society described earlier set these cultures apart from our own in respect to the particular motives involved.

infanticide

12.54 The lack of strength of the _____ and _____ motives among the Zuni is probably due to the fact that the society strongly discourages any manifestation of personal initiative.

power
status

12.55 A condition almost opposite to that of the Zuni culture is seen in the Dobu of northwestern Melanesia. These primitives are fiercely competitive and openly strive for status and power. A comparison of

the two societies indicates that the
_____ motive varies with the   status
_____.   culture (society)

12.56 Among the _____, the status   Zuni
motive is weak, while among the
_____, it is wrong.   Dobu

12.57 Variations in the motive to achieve also
occur. In some societies, such as the Arapesh of New Guinea, there is virtually
no overt expression of achievement motivation. Any behavior suggesting self-
assertiveness is discouraged. As with the
other social motives, the low degree of
achievement motivation among the Ara-   interpersonal
pesh is learned through _____   interaction
_____.

12.58 The strength of the status motive varies
widely. It is _____ among the   strong
Dobu, _____ among the Zuni.   weak

12.59 An example of affiliative motivation dif-
fering from that in our own society is
found in a society which commonly en-
courages infanticide. The achievement
motive is quite weak in the _____.   Arapesh

12.60 Thus far we have discussed the cultural
v_____ of secondary motives   variation
only. It should be noted that the mani-
festations of primary motives may also
vary with the culture. The Balinese, for
example, dislike eating, especially in pub-
lic. They thus conceal the practice as
much as possible. It is important to observe that this dislike for eating is a
modification of the manner of expression

of the hunger drive, not of the drive itself, since the hunger drive is physiological and unlearned.

12.61 It might be concluded that in the case of a secondary motive, the motive itself may vary with the culture, while in the case of a primary motive, the drive will be unchanged, but its manifestation may vary with the culture. This difference between primary and secondary motives is due to the fact that the former are

unlearned
learned

_____, while the latter are _____.

secondary
learned
interpersonal
  interaction

12.62 Social motives are _____ motives which are _____ through _____ _____.

One of the principal bases of variation in strength or type of expression of a particular secondary motive is the

culture

_____ in which the motive occurs.

12.63 Culture may cause variations in the

secondary

_____ motives but affects only the manner of expression of

primary

_____ drives.

Primary

12.64 _____ motives are universal, occurring in all cultures, while

secondary

most _____ motives probably are not.

12.65 Certain secondary motives are learned only through interpersonal interaction. Motives in this category are called

social motives

_____ _____.

UNCONSCIOUS MOTIVATION

The social motives discussed thus far have been those which would be considered to be primarily conscious in nature. That is, the individual is aware that he is motivated to affiliate or to attain higher status. Some motivation, however, is not conscious. Such unconscious motives may be manifested in normal behavior, such as slips of the tongue. They may also be the basis for abnormal behavior, as in the case of the individual who greatly fears an object which is not at all dangerous to him.

12.66 Individuals are not always conscious of the motives for their behavior. When this is true, the motivation is said to be *unconscious*.

12.67 While the individual may not know the reasons for his behavior, unconscious motives play an important part in both normal and abnormal psychology. *Freud* pointed out that certain normal behavior, such as *slips of the tongue*, may be due to the operation of powerful unconscious motives.

12.68 Slips of the tongue are one example of the influence of _____ motives on behavior. Freud held that these drives originate as powerful impulses in an unconscious part of the psychic structure called the *id*.

    unconscious

12.69 _____ _____ originate, according to Freud, in the id. These drives may cause certain normal behavior, such as _____ _____ _____ _____. They may also be the basis for abnormal conditions, such as *phobias*.

    Unconscious motives

    slips of the tongue

12.70 A phobia is an excessive fear of some act or object that is, in reality, not at all dangerous to the individual. The actual motivation for the phobia is

unconscious _____.

12.71 A famous case of phobia was Freud's (1925) case of a five-year-old boy named Hans. The real fear upon which Hans's phobia was based was his fear of the punishment he anticipated from his father. It was not, however, this fear which he expressed, but rather a morbid fear of horses on the street.

unconscious

horses

12.72 Hans's fear of his father was the _____ motivation for his behavior. The consciously expressed motive was a fear of _____.

father

12.73 The horses which were the conscious object of Hans's fear are called *phobic objects*. The *real object* of his fear motive was his _____.

father, horses

12.74 In a phobia, the fear is displaced from a real object to a phobic object. In the case of Hans, fear was displaced from his _____ to the _____.

unconscious
displaced
  phobic

12.75 The actual fear upon which a phobia is based is _____. The fear is _____ to a _____ object.

unconscious
phobia

displacement

12.76 Hans's _____ fear of his father was the basis for his _____. The process or mechanism through which this fear was expressed as a fear of horses is called _____.

THE MOTIVATION OF BEHAVIOR

When an individual displays motivated behavior, which motive is his behavior based on? Is the motive primary or secondary? Social or nonsocial? Conscious or unconscious?

Let us consider an example. A particular college student studies very hard for an examination, staying up late for several nights, cutting classes to study, etc. What is the motivation for this behavior? There are numerous possibilities. The student may have very high achievement motivation and a desire to compete with and do better than the other students in his classes; or he may have a fear of failing the exam for various reasons. He may, on the other hand, aspire to enter his chosen occupation with a company which has set high academic standards or may wish to go on to graduate school. Possibly his motivation is to please his parents, or it may be a fear of angering or shaming them by failing. Another possibility is that this student is attempting to compensate for a physical disability by excelling academically. It might even be that his motivation is a functionally autonomous derivative of a primary hunger drive which was unsatisfied in childhood because his parents were poor. Which of these motives is operating to make this particular student study? The most probable answer is that it is not any one motive but a combination of motives. In general, *most human behavior* is the result of the operation of a *complex system* of motives, each interacting with the other motives making up the system. It is for this reason that the motivation behind human behavior is often difficult to pinpoint.

12.77 Most human behavior is based not on a single motive but on a complex s_____ of motives.

system

12.78 The drives constituting a motivational system interact with each other to produce b_____.

behavior

12.79 The motivational basis for human behavior is a _____ _____ of interacting motives.

complex
system

system

12.80 The motives constituting the motivational _____ behind a particular act may vary in both *kind* and *degree* from act to act and from individual to individual.

motivational

12.81 The m_____ system which causes college student X to study may be composed of, say, high achievement motivation and a desire to please his parents. Student Y may be motivated by a somewhat lower degree of achievement motivation and by a functionally autonomous derivative of an early hunger drive. In this simplified example, the difference

degree

in achievement motivation between X and Y is one of _____. The remainder of their motivational systems differs in kind.

interaction

12.82 Human behavior is usually the result of the i_____ of the several motives comprising the motivational system behind a particular act. For a given individual, the motivational system behind one act may differ from that behind

kind
degree

another in either _____ or _____.

act
individual

12.83 The motives constituting complex systems may differ from act to _____ and from individual to _____.

kind
degree

12.84 The motives of two different individuals may differ in both _____ and _____.

12.85 The motivation for a particular act performed by a given individual is actually a number of motives which make up a _____ _____ .

complex
motivational
system

DRUG ADDICTION

12.86 The individual addicted to a narcotic, such as morphine or heroin, has, in a very real sense, a drive to obtain the drug. As was noted earlier, this special drive is difficult to place within our classification system because it is acquired, yet physiological.

12.87 The statement that drug addiction is an acquired or _____ drive is a rather obvious one, since the individual surely is not born with an intense desire for morphine. That addiction is physiological may not be so obvious. The fact that it is, however, is well established.

learned
(secondary)

12.88 When an individual begins taking a narcotic, actual *physiochemical* changes take place in his body (Noyes and Kolb, 1963). He acquires an actual physiological need for the drug. The exact mechanism of these changes is not known, although several theories have attempted to explain them.

12.89 One type of evidence that drug addiction is physiological is that actual _____ changes take place after a few doses of the drug have been taken.

physiochemical

12.90 A second and related line of evidence is that if drugs are withdrawn from an addict, there are a number of physiological changes, including pupil dilation and fever.

12.91 A third finding indicating that the addiction drive is not purely *psychological* is that lower animals become addicts. In one study, chimpanzees received morphine injections over a number of months. After several weeks of injections, failure to give an injection resulted in physiological changes and behavior suggesting desire for an injection (Spragg, 1940). This finding indicates that drug addiction is not purely p_____, but largely _____.

psychological
physiochemical

12.92 Three findings indicate that drug addiction is physiological. (1) After a few doses of the drug, there are _____ changes; (2) _____ of the drug from an addict causes physiological changes; and (3) _____ _____ can become addicted.

physiochemical
withdrawal

lower animals

12.93 The drug-addiction drive is difficult to classify because it is both l_____ and _____.

learned
   (acquired)
physiological

12.94 The drug addict has acquired a _____ _____ for the narcotic.

physiological need

12.95 The drug-addiction motive might be summarized by saying that it is a(n) _____ _____ drive.

acquired (learned)
   physiological

Motivational Theory 13

In order to understand and explain the various phenomena which are classified as aspects of motivation, it is necessary to organize these phenomena into some logical framework which can make experimentally testable predictions. Such a framework is called a *theory,* and the predictions which are made from the general theory are called *hypotheses.* If the hypotheses generated by a particular theory are supported by experimental tests, the hypotheses are said to be confirmed, and the general theory from which the hypotheses are drawn also receives partial confirmation. For any particular set of phenomena, there may be several theories extant at any given time. A case in point is the simultaneous existence of the wave and particle theories of light in physics. The multiple-theory situation also applies to motivation, where there are a number of theoretical structures, each attempting to explain and predict the same general set of phenomena.

13.1 A logical structure which relates a number
of phenomena is called a _____.   theory
In order to determine the validity of a
_____, it is necessary to gener-   theory

ate a number of hypotheses which can be tested experimentally.

hypothesis

13.2 If a _____ derived from a particular theory is supported, the theory is said to be partially confirmed.

13.3 Consider the following example of the operation of a theory. Suppose we have a general theory about handedness which predicts certain differences between right- and left-handed individuals and that the theory generates the specific

hypothesis

_____ that right-handed persons are more intelligent. In order to determine in part the validity of the theory, it would

test

be possible to t_____ the intelligence hypothesis experimentally by giving intelligence tests to right- and left-handed individuals and comparing the two groups.

13.4 In the above example, if it were found that right-handed persons were, in general, more intelligent, the hypothesis would be supported and the general theory would be

confirmed

partially _____.

theories

13.5 There are a number of _____ which attempt to explain and predict motivational phenomena. Before considering some specific viewpoints, it will be helpful to note some of the major problems facing any motivational theorist.

PROBLEMS IN MOTIVATIONAL THEORY

Before considering some specific motivational theories, it will be helpful to note some of the major problems facing any motivational theorist. For our purposes, we shall consider four such problems. The first of these is the theoretical determination of the factor or factors responsible for *drive arousal*. In general, there are two types of arousers, internal and external. The former operate within the organism to activate drives, while the latter operate in the external environment but impinge upon the organism.

A second problem involves the relative importance and specific operation of the energizing and directive functions of drive. Some theorists hold that drive, per se, has only an energizing function. Others attribute both functions to drive.

A third major topic to be considered in constructing a theory of motivation is the types of drives, i.e., primary and secondary. Several specific questions may be noted within the broad topic of drive type. The first concerns the *classification* of drives. For some drives, classification as primary or secondary is relatively easy. There is general agreement, for example, that hunger is a primary drive and that the drive to obtain money is a secondary drive. Some drives, such as *curiosity,* however, defy easy classification. There is no general agreement about whether curiosity is a primary or a secondary drive. A second major question is whether or not secondary or learned drives are permanently dependent on the satisfaction of primary drives. In our earlier discussion of this question, it was noted that some theorists believe that all secondary drives are permanently based on primary drives, while others, such as Allport, hold that secondary motives may become *functionally autonomous*.

A final consideration is the *persistence* of motives. Why are some motives more persistent than others, and why does the persistence of a given motive vary within an individual?

Drive arousal

13.6   What factor or factors are responsible for the *arousal* of drives? This is an important question which must be considered by any motivational theorist. For some drives, the answer *seems* obvious. We have noted, for example, that the hunger drive is activated by a physiological deficit or _____.   need

13.7   Possibly the deficit factor could be used

arousal

pain
external

deficit (need)
internal

internal,
external

internal

external

as a general explanation for drive _____. But what of the pain drive induced by shock? Here, it would appear that not a deficit but rather an external stimulus is responsible.

13.8 In general, there are two classes of drive arousers, which may be conveniently called *internal* factors and *external* factors. Shock, which arouses the _____ drive, is an _____ factor.

13.9 Internal factors are those which operate within the organism to activate drives, while external factors are those which impinge upon the organism. The thirst drive, which is aroused by a physiological _____, is an example of drive activated primarily by _____ factors.

13.10 Although it is possible to classify the activators of most drives into _____ and _____, the job of the drive theorist is not an easy one. Many of the drive-arousing factors are not known, and in some cases, particularly with secondary drives, there may be several factors operating simultaneously.

13.11 The physiological need which arouses the hunger drive is _____, while the stimulus activating the pain drive is _____.

13.12 The major point of the above discussion is that any drive theory must endeavor

to explain and predict the _____   arousal
of drives.

13.13   What are the two types of factors (in
any order) which arouse drives?
(1) _____   (1) internal
(2) _____   (2) external

Energizing and directing functions of drives

13.14   It was noted in our earlier discussion of
drives that two primary properties often
associated with drives are the *energizing*
and the *direction* of behavior. Unfortunately, theorists have been unable to
agree on the relative importance and
operation of these two functions.

13.15   A rat deprived of food for forty-eight
hours is more active than a nondeprived
rat, indicating that the hunger drive has
energized the rat's behavior. Some psychologists, such as Brown and Farber
(1955), hold that the function of the
drive, per se, stops here. That is, it only
_____ the animal's behavior.   energizes

13.16   If the rat has previously learned that a
bar press will bring food, the rat will
perform the response when deprived of
food. It might thus be held that the
hunger drive also *directs* behavior.

13.17   Brown and Farber reject the directive
function and ascribe it to factors other
than the d_____. Thus, for   drive
these theorists the only function of a
drive is to _____ behavior.   energize

13.18 Other psychologists, such as Bindra (1959) and Young (1961), hold that a drive both energizes and directs behavior. The latter function is ascribed to the drive because it activates instrumental behavior leading to specific goals which reduce the drive.

instrumental

directs

13.19 When the rat bar-presses for food, it is performing i_____ behavior. If the immediate cause of this specific behavior is the hunger drive, we can say that the drive _____ behavior.

energizes

energizes
directs

13.20 Brown and Farber hypothesize that a drive only _____ behavior, while Young and Bindra hold that the drive both _____ and _____ behavior.

13.21 The energy-direction question has generally been considered by motivational theorists to be an important one. It is a question with no easy answer, and only further research can give a solution.

energizing

directive

13.22 The major theorists involved in the drive-function controversy described above agree that drives do have an _____ function.

13.23 The controversy is over the _____ function of drives.

They theorize
that the only
function of a
drive is to
energize
behavior.

13.23a Describe briefly the Brown-Farber viewpoint.

_____
_____
_____
_____

13.23b Describe briefly Bindra's viewpoint.

_____

_____

_____

_____

Bindra believes
that a drive
both energizes
and directs
behavior.

13.24 The energy-direction question has been handled in various ways by different theorists and has generally been incorporated into the larger theoretical structure. The important point is that the question must be dealt with by any complete motivational theory.

Primary and secondary drives

13.25 A third major topic to be considered in constructing a theory of motivation is the types of drives, i.e., primary and secondary.

13.26 Several specific questions may be noted within the broad topic of drive type. The first concerns the *classification* of drives. For some drives, classification as primary or secondary is relatively easy. There is general agreement, for example, that hunger is a primary drive and that the drive to obtain money is a secondary drive. Some drives, such as *curiosity*, however, defy easy classification.

13.27 There is no general agreement about whether curiosity is a primary or a secondary drive. A second major question is whether or not secondary or learned drives are permanently dependent on the satisfaction of primary drives. In our earlier discussion of this question, it was noted that some theorists believe that all secondary drives are permanently based on primary drives, while others, such as Allport, hold that secondary motives may become *functionally autonomous.*

functionally
autonomous

13.28 If a secondary motive becomes independent of any physiological drive, the secondary motive is said to be _____ _____.
Whether or not this condition occurs is a major question for motivational theory.

13.29 Two major theoretical questions concern the *classification* of drives as primary or secondary and the possibility of a secondary drive becoming _____ _____.

functionally
autonomous

13.30 A third question concerns the mechanism or mechanisms for the learning of secondary drives. Is the mechanism the same for all drives, or do several mechanisms act in combination?

mechanisms

13.31 Although it is agreed that secondary drives are learned, the _____ of learning are not known.

theory

13.32 In constructing a _____ of motivation, the mechanism of learning secondary drives should be considered.

13.33 The three questions concerning primary and secondary drives are: (1) the _____ of drives; (2) the validity of the hypothesis that secondary drives are based on _____

classification

_____; and (3) the mecha-   primary drives
nisms for the _____ of   learning
_____ drives.   secondary

13.34 It is generally agreed that the
       drive to obtain poker chips which
       may be developed in chimpanzees
       is a _____ drive. The   secondary
       _____ of learning is, how-   mechanism
       ever, in doubt.

13.34a State the three major questions (in any
       order) concerning primary and secon-
       dary drives.
       (1) _____   (1) classification of
                                                  drives
       (2) _____   (2) the validity of
           _____   the hypothesis
           _____   that secondary
           _____   drives are
           _____   based on
           _____   primary
           _____   drives
       (3) _____   (3) the mechanisms
           _____   for the learn-
           _____   ing of secon-
           _____   dary drives

13.35 The problem of classifying drives as
       _____ or _____   primary, secondary
       must be considered by a motivational
       theorist.

   Persistence of motives
13.36 A final problem to be noted is the fact
       that some motives are more *persistent*
       than others and that persistence of a
       given motive varies with the individual.

13.37 If a rat is given continuous electric shock or a series of brief shocks, it will continue to show avoidance behavior (e.g., pressing a bar to avoid shock) as long as the shock continues. The behavior resulting from the activation of the pain drive thus shows great _____ .

persistence

13.38 A rat deprived of food will become more active up to a deprivation time of about sixty hours (Yamaguchi, 1951). After this amount of time, the rat weakens, and activity decreases until the animal eventually dies. Since activity increases and then decreases, we might say that the hunger drive is somewhat less _____ than the pain drive.

persistent

13.39 In the examples discussed above, persistence varied as a function of type of _____ . Thus, the same animal might exhibit greater persistence in behavior initiated by the _____ drive than in _____ -motivated behavior.

drive

pain
hunger

13.40 Since the pain drive produces more prolonged instrumental activity than does hunger, the pain drive is more _____ .

persistent

13.41 Differences in persistence also occur between different individuals experiencing the same drive. This is especially true of secondary drives.

13.42 Two young men, John and Tom, both have a desire to become doctors. When it is found that relative poverty and great hardships must be endured to achieve this goal, however, Tom may decide to enter another profession, while John may go to medical school despite the hardships. In this case, we might say that Tom's drive to become a doctor is less _____ than is John's.

persistent

13.43 It has been pointed out that there may be differences in persistence between different _____ or between different _____ experiencing the same drive.

drives
individuals

13.44 If it is agreed that there are variations in persistence, the motivational theorist is faced with the problem of accounting for these differences within his logical framework. He should also consider possible mechanisms to account for the differences. Primary drives may vary in persistence as a function of degree of deprivation (hunger, thirst), strength of noxious stimulation (pain), past experience of the organism, etc. Persistence of secondary drives may depend on the strength of original learning, amount of reinforcement given during the learning of the drive, or the individual's need for the particular goal of the drive. These are only a few of the possible factors that may be involved. The important point is that differences in persistence do occur and should be considered in formulating a theory of motivation.

13.45 Four major topics to be considered in motivational theories have been dis-

arousal

energizing,
directing

primary
secondary
persistence

cussed. They include: (1) drive _____; (2) the drive function controversy, which involves the _____ and _____ functions of drives; (3) the problems which are concerned with the differentiation of drives into two types, i.e., _____ and _____; and (4) differences in the _____ of motivated behavior.

classification

13.46 Within the topic of drive type, it was pointed out that three problems deserve consideration: (1) the _____ of drives as primary and secondary; (2) the validity of the hypothesis that secondary drives may become independent of primary drives, i.e., become

functionally
autonomous
learning

_____ _____; and (3) the mechanisms for the _____ of secondary drives.

(1) drive arousal
(2) energy-direction controversy
(3) primary-
    secondary
    differentiation
(4) drive
    persistence
Subdivisions:
  (1) drive
      classification
  (2) functional-
      autonomy
      hypothesis
  (3) learning
      mechanism

13.47 State (in any order) the four major problems facing the motivational theorist and the three subdivisions of the drive-type problem.

_____
_____
_____
_____
_____
_____
_____
_____
_____
_____
_____
_____
_____

DEFICIENCY MOTIVATION

Having considered the phenomena of concern to motivational theorists, it is now appropriate to consider some specific theories. Since it would be impossible to discuss all the numerous theories of motivation, three major viewpoints have been chosen because they represent the principal trends of current motivational theorizing and because each general viewpoint has within its scope several specific theories. Three general viewpoints, deficiency motivation, growth motivation, and hedonism, will be considered briefly.

13.48 The deficiency viewpoint simply holds that instrumental behavior results from a need, which represents a *deficit*. The reader may recognize this viewpoint as the one often stressed in the present text. It has been stressed not because it is necessarily more valid but because it has been developed in more detail and was more readily adaptable to the purposes of this book. Since the theory has already been covered in some detail throughout the text, it is necessary here only to reiterate several major points and to mention some criticisms of the theory.

13.49 According to the deficit theory, the hunger drive and the consequent instrumental behavior are initiated by a _____. Behavior relative to a given motive occurs in a *cycle* from disequilibrium to equilibrium. The postulated cycle was presented previously in Chapter I.

need (deficit)

13.50 The hunger drive is activated by a physiological _____ and satiated by reaching a goal through instrumental behavior. Further deprivation again acti-

need (deficit)

cyclical

vates the drive. The deficit viewpoint thus holds that motivation is _____.

13.51 The cyclical nature of motivation is a major postulate of the _____ theory. Thirst, according to this theory, is based on a _____ for water.

deficit

need

13.52 A second major postulate of the deficit theory is that secondary motives are based on primary motives. The implications of this postulate have been discussed in connection with functional autonomy.

13.53 The hypothesis that the drive to obtain money is based on an earlier drive to obtain food is consistent with the _____ theory of motivation.

deficit

13.54 The deficiency viewpoint holds that secondary drives are _____ on primary drives. An alternative viewpoint discussed earlier states that a secondary drive may be _____.

based

functionally
autonomous

13.55 The basic postulate of the deficiency theory is that any drive and the consequent instrumental behavior are activated by a _____.

need (deficit)

13.56 Some psychologists have criticized the deficiency viewpoint. The principal objection is that it does not explain all motivated behavior. The critics point out that if only deficits motivate behavior, individuals whose basic physiological drives are constantly satisfied would never change or develop. They would have no vigor and would be almost entirely inactive. The satiated condition would certainly seem to apply to most middle-class Americans; yet, these individuals often strive diligently to obtain money, social status, prestige, etc. What is their motivation? Surely such behavior is not due to physiological deficit.

13.57 State (in any order) three of the major postulates of deficiency theory:

(1) _____

_____

(2) _____

_____

(3) _____

_____

_____

(1) Need activates drive.
(2) Motivation is cyclical.
(3) Secondary drives are based on primary drives.

13.58 Critics of the deficiency theory point out that some behavior does not appear to be motivated by physiological _____. Arguments pro and con have been extensively developed. It is not, however, our purpose to discuss the topic in detail here, but only to note the controversy.

deficits
(needs)

GROWTH MOTIVATION

13.59 Critics of the deficiency theory, such as Maslow (1955), are often proponents of a viewpoint known as *growth* motivation.

13.60 Where deficiency theory proposes negative motivation, growth theory proposes _____ motivation. The individual is motivated, according to growth theory, to grow and to develop his *potentialities*.

positive

deficiency

potentialities

13.61 According to growth theory, no d_____ need be present for the individual to exhibit motivated behavior. An individual may be motivated to develop his _____.

13.62 One of the foremost proponents of growth theory, Maslow (1955), postulates that the highest form of motivation is *self-actualization*. As opposed to deficiency motivation, self-actualization involves

positive

_____ motivation. It means simply that an individual strives to become that for which he is suited.

13.63 Maslow proposes that after the individual's physiological needs and lower secondary drives are satisfied, he reaches the highest form of motivation,

self-actualization

_____.

13.64 Self-actualization is seen as the organism's tendency to realize its

potentialities
negative
positive

_____. Where deficiency motivation is _____, growth motivation is _____.

13.65 Other proponents of growth motivation have included Goldstein (1939, 1947) and Rogers (1951). Like Maslow, these theorists propose that the individual is motivated primarily not by a series of

needs
potentialities
self-actualization

_____ but by a tendency to realize his _____, i.e., by a tendency toward _____.

13.66 A basic difference between the growth and deficiency viewpoints is that

positive

the former postulates _____

motivation, while the latter stresses
_____ motivation.   negative

13.67 Self-actualization is the organism's tendency to _____ its _____.   realize,
According to Maslow, it is the highest   potentialities
form of motivation.

HEDONISM

13.68 The hedonistic theory of motivation is the
oldest and perhaps the simplest of the
three viewpoints discussed here. It dates
at least to the Greek philosophers,
particularly the Cyrenaics and Epicureans,
and has passed through several periods
of popularity and decline. At the present
time, its popularity appears to be rising.
Basically, the theory states that the
organism strives to *attain pleasure* and
to *avoid pain*.

13.69 Unlike the deficiency and growth theories,
hedonism gives no primary importance to
either deficiencies or a tendency to
realize capacities. It says simply that
if a particular state is unpleasant, the
organism will strive to change or leave
that state but that if the state is
_____, the organism will strive   pleasant
to attain or maintain the state.

13.70 _____ theory holds that food   Deficiency
deprivation creates a physiological need
which instigates a drive to obtain food.
The hedonistic theory says, however, that
deprivation creates a condition which is
perceived by the organism as an unpleasant state to be corrected by obtain-
ing food.

13.71 Young (1961) found that human beings deprived of food or water report that they experience an unpleasant state. The experiment thus supports the _____ viewpoint.

hedonistic

13.72 American hedonists have included Thorndike, Young, and McClelland. Although their theories differ in details, the basic postulate of each is that the organism strives to _____ _____ and _____ _____.

attain pleasure
avoid pain

13.73 The three viewpoints of motivation discussed are the: _____, _____, and _____ viewpoints.

deficiency
growth,
hedonistic

13.74 The oldest theory of the three is the hedonistic theory. The _____ theory postulates negative motivation, while the _____ theory postulates positive motivation. It should be noted that the _____ theory postulates both positive and negative motivations.

deficiency

growth

hedonistic

13.75 The three viewpoints presented here have been discussed only in skeleton form. Specific variations of the general theories have not been discussed, although it is noted that in each case there are several variations. The reader will also note that no attempt has been made to evaluate the various theories in terms of experimental evidence, since such an evaluation is beyond the scope of this text. Finally, it should be noted that certain theories of motivation would fall into none of the categories that have been discussed here.

Bibliography

Adolph, E. F. The internal environment and behavior: water content. *Amer. J. Psychiat.*, 1941, **6**, 1365–1373.

Allport, G. W. *Personality: a psychological interpretation.* New York: Holt, 1937.

Andersson, B., & McCann, S. M. A further study of polydipsia evolved by hypothalamic stimulation in the goat. *Acta physiol. Scand.*, 1955, **33**, 333–346.

Andersson, B., & McCann, S. M. The effect of hypothalamic lesions on the water intake of the dog. *Acta physiol. Scand.*, 1956, **35**, 312–320.

Atkinson, J. W. Studies in projective measurement of achievement motivation. Unpublished doctoral dissertation, University of Michigan, 1950. Cited by D. C. McClelland, J. W. Atkinson, R. A. Clark, & E. L. Lowell, *The achievement motive.* New York: Appleton-Century-Crofts, 1953.

Atkinson, J. W. Motivational determinants of risk-taking behavior. *Psychol. Rev.*, 1957, **64**, 359–372.

Atkinson, J. W., & Litwin, G. H. Achievement motive and test anxiety conceived as motive to approach success and motive to avoid failure. *J. abnorm. soc. Psychol.*, 1960, **60**, 52–63.

Bartoshuk, A. Electromyographic gradients as indicants of motivation. *Canad. J. Psychol.*, 1955, **9**, 215–230.

160

Beach, F. A. Importance of progesterone to induction of sexual receptivity in spayed female rats. *Proc. soc. exp. Biol. Med.*, 1942, **51**, 369–371.

Beach, F. A. A review of physiological and psychological studies of sexual behavior in mammals. *Physiol. Rev.*, 1947, **27**, 240–307.

Bellows, R. T. Time factors in water drinking in dogs. *Amer. J. Physiol.*, 1939, **125**, 87–97.

Benedict, Ruth. *Patterns of culture.* Boston: Houghton Mifflin, 1934.

Bindra, D. *Motivation: a systematic reinterpretation.* New York: Ronald, 1959.

Birney, R. C., Burdick, H., & Teevan, R. C. Motive correlates of achievement aspiration strategies. Paper read at Eastern Psychol. Ass. Philadelphia, 1960.

Birney, R. C., Burdick, H., & Teevan, R. C. A theory of achievement behavior. Unpublished manuscript, Bucknell University, 1964.

Brobeck, J. R. Mechanism of the development of obesity in animals with hypothalamic lesions. *Physiol. Rev.*, 1946, **26**, 541–559.

Brookhart, J. M., & Dey, F. L. Reduction of sexual behavior in male guinea pigs by hypothalamic lesions. *Amer. J. Physiol.*, 1941, **133**, 551–554.

Brown, J. S., & Farber, I. E. Emotions conceptualized as intervening variables—with suggestions toward a theory of frustration. *Psychol. Bull.*, 1951, **48**, 465–495.

Campbell, D., Sanderson, R. E., & Laverty, S. G. Characteristics of a conditioned response in human subjects during extinction trials following a single traumatic conditioning trial. *J. abnorm. soc. Psychol.*, 1964, **68** (6), 627–639.

Cannon, W. B. *The wisdom of the body.* New York: Norton, 1932.

Cannon, W. B. Hunger and thirst. In C. Murchison (ed.), *A handbook of general experimental psychology.* Worchester, Mass.: Clark Univer. Press, 1934. Pp. 247–263.

Clark, R. A., & McClelland, D. C. A factor analytic integration of imaginative, performance, and case study measures of need for achievement. Unpublished paper, 1950. Cited by D. C. McClelland, J. W. Atkinson, R. A. Clark, & E. L. Lowell, *The achievement motive.* New York: Appleton-Century-Crofts, 1953.

Clauberg, C., & Schultze, K. W. Die Folgen der sterilisierung und der kastration bei Mann und frau. *S. F. arztl. Fot.*, 1934, **31**, 425.

Cowles, J. T. Food tokens as incentives for learning by chimpanzees. *Comp. psychol. Monogr.*, 1937, **14**, No. 5.

Daniel, R. S., & Smith, K. U. The sea-approach behavior of the neonate loggerhead turtle (caretta caretta). *J. comp. physiol. Psychol.*, 1947, **40**, 413–420.

Davis, C. M. Self-selection of diet by newly weaned infants. *Amer. J. dis. Child*, 1928, **36**, 651–679.

Delgado, J. M. R., & Anand, B. K. Increase of food intake induced by electrical stimulation of the lateral hypothalamus. *Amer. J. Physiol.,* 1953, **172,** 162–168.

Ford, C. S., & Beach, F. A. *Patterns of sexual behavior.* New York: Harper & Row, 1952.

Frank, R. T. *The female sex hormones.* Baltimore: Thomas, 1929.

Freud, S. *Collected Papers,* Vol. III. International Psychoanalytic Press, London, 1925.

Goldstein, K. *The organism, a holistic approach to biology derived from pathological data in man.* New York: American Book, 1939.

Goldstein, K. *Organismic approach to the problem of motivation.* Trans. New York: New York Academy of Sciences, 1947, **9,** 218–230.

Hancock, J., & Teevan, R. C. Fear of failure and risk-taking behavior. Tech. Rpt. No. 4, Office of Naval Research, 1964.

Hess, E. H. Imprinting. *Science,* 1959, **130,** 133–141.

Heyns, R. W., Veroff, J., & Atkinson, J. W. A scoring manual for the affiliation motive. In J. W. Atkinson (ed.), *Motives in fantasy, action, and society.* New York: Van Nostrand, 1958.

Holmes, J. H., & Gregersen, M. I. Relation of the salivary flow to the thirst produced in man by intravenous injection of hypertonic salt solution. *Amer. J. Physiol.,* 1947, **151,** 252–257.

James, W. *The principles of psychology.* New York: Holt, 1890.

Lindsley, D. B., Bowden, J., & Magoun, H. W. Effect upon the EEG of acute injury to the brain stem activating system. *EEG clin. Neurophysiol.,* 1949, **1,** 475–486.

Luckhardt, G., & Carlson, A. Contributions to the physiology of the stomach: XVII. On the chemical control of the gastric hunger mechanism. *Amer. J. Physiol.,* 1914, **36,** 37–46.

McClelland, D. C., Atkinson, J. W., Clark, R. A., & Lowell, E. L. *The achievement motive.* New York: Appleton-Century-Crofts, 1953.

McDougall, W. *An introduction to social psychology.* Boston: J. W. Luce, 1926.

Maslow, A. H. *Motivation and personality.* New York: Harper & Row, 1954.

Maslow, A. H. Deficiency motivation and growth motivation. In M. R. Jones (ed.), *Nebraska Symposium on Motivation.* Lincoln, Neb.: University of Nebraska Press, 1955.

Melzack, R. The perception of pain. *Sci. Amer.,* 1961, **204** (2), 41–49.

Miller, N. E. Studies of fear as an acquirable drive: I. Fear as motivation and fear-reduction as reinforcement in the learning of new responses. *J. exp. Psychol.,* 1948, **38,** 89–101.

Miller, N. E. Learnable drives and rewards. In S. S. Stevens (ed.), *Handbook of experimental psychology.* New York: Wiley, 1951.

Miller, N. E. *Subcortical integrative mechanisms.* In D. E. Sheer (ed.), *Electrical stimulation of the brain.* Austin, Tex.: University of Texas Press, 1957.

Miller, N. E. Central stimulation and other new approaches to motivation and reward. *Amer. Psychologist,* 1958, **13**, 100–108.

Montgomery, M. F. The role of salivary glands in the thirst mechanism. *Amer. J. Psychol.,* 1931, **96**, 221–227.

Moruzzi, G., & Magoun, H. W. Brain stem reticular formation and activation of the EEG. *EEG clin. Neurophysiol.,* 1949, **1**, 455–473.

Moulton, R. W. Notes for a projective measure of fear of failure. In J. W. Atkinson (ed.), *Motives in fantasy, action, and society.* Princeton, N.J.: Van Nostrand, 1958.

Noyes, A. P., & Kolb, L. C. *Modern clinical psychiatry.* Philadelphia: Saunders, 1963.

Olds, J. *Physiological mechanisms of reward.* In M. R. Jones (ed.), *Nebraska Symposium on Motivation.* Lincoln, Nebr.: University of Nebraska Press, 1955. Pp. 73–139.

Olds, J. A preliminary mapping of electrical reinforcing effects in the rat brain. *J. comp. physiol. Psychol.,* 1956, **49**, 281–285.

Olds, J. Self-stimulation of the brain. *Science,* 1958, **127**, 315–323.

Quigley, J. P., Johnson, N., & Solomon, E. I. Action of insulin on the motility of the gastrointestinal tract. *Amer. J. Physiol.,* 1929, **90**, 89–98.

Richter, C. P. Increased salt appetite in adrenalectomized rats. *Amer. J. Physiol.,* 1936, **115**, 155–161.

Richter, C. P. Total self-regulatory functions in animals and human beings. *Harvey Lectures,* 1942–1943, **30**, 63–103.

Rogers, C. R. *Client-centered therapy; its current practice, implications, and theory.* Boston: Houghton Mifflin, 1951.

Root, W. S., & Bard, P. Erection in the cat following removal of lumbrosacral segments. *Amer. J. Physiol.,* 1937, **119**, 392–393.

Seward, J. P. Studies on the reproductive activities of the guinea pig: III. The effect of androgenic hormone on sex drive in males and females. *J. comp. Psychol.,* 1940, **30**, 435–449.

Sheffield, F. D., & Roby, T. B. Reward values of a non-nutritive sweet taste. *J. comp. physiol. Psychol.,* 1950, **43**, 471–481.

Smith, B. D., & Teevan, R. C. The relationship of hostile press and need achievement to measures of self-ideal congruence and adjustment. Tech. Rpt. No. 10, Office of Naval Research, 1964.

Smith, O. A. Food intake and hypothalamic stimulation. In D. E. Sheer (ed.), *Electrical stimulation of the brain.* Austin, Tex.: University of Texas Press, 1961. Pp. 367–370.

Solomon, R. L., & Wynne, L. C. Traumatic avoidance learning: acquisition in normal dogs. *Psychol. Monogr.*, 1953, **67**, No. 354.

Spragg, S. D. Morphine injection in chimpanzees. *Comp. psychol. Monogr.*, 1940, **15**, No. 7.

Steggerda, F. R. Observations on the water intake in an adult man with dysfunctioning salivary glands. *Amer. J. Physiol.*, 1941, **132**, 517–521.

Stone, C. P. Copulatory activity in adult male rats following castration and injections of testosterone propionate. *Endocrinology*, 1939, **24**, 165–174. (*a*)

Stone, C. P. Sex drive. In E. A. Allen (ed.), *Sex and internal secretions.* Baltimore: Williams & Wilkins, 1939. (*b*)

Teevan, R. C., & Hartsough, R. W. Personality correlates of fear of failure and need for achievement: I. Values scales. Tech. Rept. No. 5, Office of Naval Research, 1964. (*a*)

Teevan, R. C., & Hartsough, R. W. Personality correlates of fear of failure and need for achievement: II. A clinical picture. Tech. Rept. No. 6, Office of Naval Research, 1964. (*b*)

Tietelbaum, P., & Stellar, E. Recovery from the failure to eat produced by hypothalamic lesions. *Science*, 1954, **120**, 894–895.

Tinbergen, N. The curious behavior of the stickleback. *Sci. Amer.*, 1952, **182**, 22–26.

Tsang, Y. C. Hunger motivation in gastrectomized rats. *J. comp. Psychol.*, 1938, **26**, 1–17.

Wangensteen, O. H., & Carlson, A. J. Hunger sensations in a patient after total gastrectomy. *Proc. soc. exp. Biol.*, 1931, **28**, 545–547.

Watson, J. B., & Rayner, R. Conditioned emotional reactions. *J. exp. Psychol.*, 1920, **3**, 1–14.

Wilder, C. E. Selection of rachitic and antirachitic diets in the rat. *J. comp. Psychol.*, 1937, **24**, 547–577.

Wilkins, G. H. *Undiscovered Australia.* New York: Putnam, 1929.

Wolfe, J. B. Effectiveness of token-rewards for chimpanzees. *Comp. psychol. Monogr.*, 1936, **12**, No. 5.

Yamaguchi, M. Drive (D) as a function of hours of hunger (h). *J. exp. Psychol.*, 1951, **42**, 108–117.

Yerkes, R. M., & Elder, J. H. Oestrous, receptivity, and mating in the chimpanzee. *Comp. psychol. Monogr.*, 1936, **13**, No. 65.

Young, P. T. Food preferences and the regulation of eating. *J. comp. Psychol.*, 1933, **15**, 167–176.

Young, P. T. *Motivation and emotion.* New York: Wiley, 1961.

Name Index

Adolph, E. F., 37, 38
Allport, G. W., 122, 123, 143, 148
Anand, B. K., 79
Anderson, B., 81
Atkinson, J. W., 113, 114, 116–119

Bard, P., 45
Bartoshuk, A., 89
Beach, F. A., 49, 53, 54
Bellows, R. T., 137
Benedict, Ruth, 132
Bindra, D., 146, 147
Birney, R. C., 119, 120
Bowden, J., 92
Brobeck, J. R., 79
Brown, J. S., 145, 146
Burdick, H., 119, 120

Campbell, D., 109, 110
Cannon, W. B., 19, 20, 28, 30, 34, 35, 67

Carlson, A., 29, 30
Clark, R. A., 113, 114, 116–118
Clauberg, C., 53
Cowles, J. T., 103

Daniel, R. S., 73
Davis, C. M., 32, 52
Delgado, J. M. R., 79

Elder, J. H., 51

Farber, I. E., 145, 146
Ford, C. S., 49
Frank, R. T., 53
Freud, S., 66–68, 135, 136

Goldstein, K., 156
Gregersen, M. I., 36

Subject Index